DATE DUE

June 28			
Aug 27			

The OVERCOMING BULIMIA

WORKBOOK

Your Comprehensive,

Step-by-Step

Guide to Recovery

RANDI E. McCABE, PH.D. • TRACI L. McFARLANE, PH.D.

MARION P. OLMSTED, PH.D.

New Harbinger Publications, Inc.

Distributed in Canada by Raincoast Books

Copyright © 2003 by Randi E. McCabe, Traci L. McFarlane, and Marion P. Olmsted
New Harbinger Publications, Inc.
5674 Shattuck Avenue
Oakland, CA 94609

Cover design by Amy Shoup
Edited by Brady Kahn
Text design by Tracy Marie Carlson

ISBN 1-57224-326-0 Paperback

Printed in the United States of America

New Harbinger Publications' Web site address: www.newharbinger.com

08   07   06

10   9   8   7   6   5

Contents

Acknowledgments

We thank our many colleagues at the Toronto General Hospital Eating Disorder Program and the Department of Psychology at St. Joseph's Healthcare for creating an environment that promotes creative thought, the free exchange of ideas, and a persistent focus on helping our clients. We especially thank Lynda Molleken, Jan Lackstrom, Susan Chudzik, and Judy King for their comments on earlier drafts of chapters. A heartfelt thank you goes to the clients who have shared their stories with us and made this book possible. We would also like to express our gratitude to Catharine Sutker and the staff at New Harbinger Publications for their support throughout the stages of developing this book.

Finally, a thank you to Lilly Kerto, Lisa DiNardo, Marty Antony, Ted Guloien, Dax Urbszat, and William Harper for their ongoing support and assistance in writing this book; we couldn't have done it without you.

Introduction

Is this book for you?

* Are you constantly preoccupied with thoughts about food?

* Does the number on the scale determine how you feel; how you will handle your day; your worth as a person?

* Do you try and control your body weight?

* Do you battle between depriving yourself of food and uncontrollable urges to eat?

* Is your life being controlled by your eating or feelings about your body?

If you answered "yes" to any of these questions, it is likely that this book will benefit you in some way.

Most people don't set out to have an eating disorder. Generally, an eating disorder develops in a gradual way. You may have started out just trying to lose a few pounds as a way of feeling better about yourself. Losing weight is a quick way to get positive attention from others. You may have heard, "You look great! Did you lose weight?" from many people. This positive attention is reinforcing and fuels the drive to feel better on the inside by changing the way you look on the outside. In the beginning, you may have felt good about the control you were taking over your eating and your weight. But it doesn't take long before the negative effects of an eating disorder kick in, and before long, you find that you are no longer controlling your life with your eating disorder. Rather, your eating disorder is controlling you.

You may feel stuck. If you start to give up your eating disorder, you may feel like you are losing control. On the other hand, if you stay where you are, you are in a constant struggle with eating disorder symptoms. This struggle is the very reason it is so hard to recover. That is where this book comes in. We can help you take a big step toward recovery. Whether you have never had any treatment for your eating disorder or you have tried lots of different types of treatment, it doesn't matter. This book will be helpful to you, wherever you are on the recovery journey.

Ten Ways This Book Will Help

You may be wondering, "How is reading a book going to help me?" That's a good question, but this book involves more than just reading and taking in information. It will help you in the following ways:

1. You will learn about your eating disorder and gain a better understanding of the role it plays in your life, including the benefits and costs.

2. You will become more aware of your eating disorder symptoms, their triggers and the emotional consequences.

3. You will gain an understanding of what factors led to the development of your eating disorder and what factors help to maintain it.

4. You will learn about normalized eating (having at least three well-balanced meals per day) and strategies to prevent bingeing.

5. You will develop a toolbox of strategies to help you decrease other eating disorder symptoms, such as vomiting, taking laxatives, and excessive exercising.

6. You will learn how to identify eating disorder thoughts and become skilled at shifting your thoughts to a more helpful, balanced style of thinking.

7. You will learn strategies to help you start to feel better about your body and decrease your feelings of body dissatisfaction.

8. You will learn strategies to build your self-worth and to tackle some of the underlying issues that may be playing a role in your eating disorder.

9. You will identify other problems in your life that may be related to your eating disorder, and you may use the strategies that you develop as you work through this book to start tackling these problems as well.

10. You will learn how to hang onto the gains you make.

How to Use This Book

There are a number of ways to use this book; the way you use it will depend on your readiness to start on the recovery journey. By just reading, you will gain a better understanding of the role your eating disorder plays in your life and the different components involved in recovery. To move forward in the recovery process, however, you will need to do more than just read. You will need to actually work. That is, you will need to practice the strategies that we suggest and try them out in your day-to-day life. The worksheets provided in each chapter will help you put the strategies that you read about into actual practice. They are the tools that will help you change.

This book is designed to take you through the different stages in the recovery process. This may be enough to make lasting changes and gain back control of your life, or it may just be one step in a larger treatment effort. If you are finding it difficult to try the strategies we suggest here, you may need a more intensive treatment approach. If this is the case, then you should seek the additional help of an eating disorder professional, a psychologist, psychiatrist, social worker, or therapist trained in the treatment of eating disorders. If you are unsure of where to find an eating disorder professional, a good place to start is with your family doctor, who will be able to tell you about the options.

Changing What's Inside

An eating disorder is all about controlling what is going on with the outside (your weight or your eating) as an attempt to feel better on the inside. Trying to change how you feel inside by changing your weight may have helped you feel good initially, but in the long run it doesn't work. This book will help you start to change the inside and help you start to feel better about yourself and to take back control of your life.

Sometimes making a change means that you feel worse before you feel better. As you begin to take control back from your eating disorder, be prepared to feel worse at times. This is a period of transition, before you have developed healthy coping strategies to replace the unhealthy ones that you've given up. Hang in there! Just remember all of the reasons why you picked up this book in the first place, and remind yourself that these are the reasons why you are going to continue on your recovery path.

A Final Note

We are psychologists who are experienced in treating individuals suffering from eating disorders, as well as in training other health professionals to treat eating disorders. Throughout this workbook, we have used examples of actual cases to help illustrate concepts and to provide context. The cases that we describe are based on the many patients we have seen for treatment over the years. Specific details have been altered to protect the privacy of individuals.

We have used the female pronoun "she" throughout because bulimia is much more common in women. However, bulimia can affect men as well, and we do give some male examples.

Chapter 1

What Is Bulimia?

Bulimia nervosa is an eating disorder that affects about 1 to 3 percent of women and girls (American Psychiatric Association 2000). That means up to three out of every one hundred females are struggling with this problem. Although this eating disorder is much more common in women, men can also develop bulimia. Bulimia most often begins in adolescence, but it can develop at any age, and it is most common in industrialized countries where food is readily available and where being thin is part of being beautiful or attractive. The course of bulimia is highly variable. Some people have bulimia at one point in their lives and then achieve a full recovery. Other people have recurring episodes of bulimia, especially during times of stress. Finally, there are some people who struggle with bulimia every day for many, many years. This chapter will help you understand what bulimia is, what symptoms you may be experiencing, and the psychological and physical consequences of bulimia. People are at different stages in their readiness to deal with their bulimia, and in this chapter you will be able to determine what stage you are at in starting the recovery process. You will also explore the role that bulimia plays in your life.

Jill's Story

Jill developed bulimia at age sixteen after she developed a bad virus that knocked her out for several weeks. Jill was an excellent athlete, and participating in sports was very important to her self-image. Prior to being ill, she exercised daily, training for the competitive track and volleyball teams. When she became ill, she was unable to train for a couple of months. During this time, she gained about ten pounds and her self-image suffered. When she was well again, she began a strict diet to lose the weight that she had gained. As her weight decreased, she received many compliments from people around her. She started to feel better about herself and decided to continue to diet and watch her weight.

Over time, Jill's diet became more restrictive. After several months, she found that it became more difficult to follow her diet, especially in the evening. She began to sneak out of the house to eat. She would go to drive-through restaurants, order a couple of meals, and eat the food in her car. Once she started eating, she felt out of control, like she couldn't stop. On a typical night, she would have two double cheeseburgers, two large fries, two large sodas, an order of chicken fingers, a milkshake, and a half dozen donuts. She would stop eating when she felt so full that she could not eat another bite. Then she would find a private bathroom, often in the donut shop, where she would vomit until she felt empty.

This pattern of eating continued for a number of years until Jill felt she could no longer go on this way. She felt she had no control over her life. Her family had noticed that she was unhappy and stressed, although they didn't know why. She kept her problem a secret and felt too ashamed to tell anyone.

Jill's story is a classic example of how bulimia can take over your life.

The Symptoms of Bulimia

The very first step in recovery from bulimia involves understanding the symptoms you are experiencing. Bulimia nervosa involves the following symptoms:

* regular episodes of binge eating

* eating binges that are followed by compensating behaviors to prevent weight gain (vomiting, laxative abuse, overexercise, and fasting)

* self-evaluation (how you feel about yourself as a person) that is largely determined by shape and weight (American Psychiatric Association 2000).

Each of these symptoms is explained in detail in the next part of this chapter.

What Is a Binge?

There are two types of binges that can occur with bulimia nervosa: objective and subjective binges.

Objective Binge

An *objective binge* involves eating, within a specific period of time (usually less than two hours), an amount of food that is considered large compared to what most people would eat in the same situation. For example, an objective binge for Jenice, a thirty-five-year-old accountant, consisted of three bowls of cereal with milk, a container of ice cream, a large bag of chips, two dozen cookies, and a bottle of soda. Most people would agree that this does not look like a normal meal or snack. As well as eating an objectively large amount of food, for an episode to qualify as a binge, a person must feel a loss of control over her eating. Eating a large amount of food without feeling any loss of control is not considered a binge. It's just overeating. But, when Jenice binged she had the feeling that she was unable to stop herself even if she wanted to. She also felt she couldn't control how much she ate. She kept going until she was physically unable to eat anymore.

Subjective Binge

A *subjective binge* occurs when a person eats and feels out of control, but the amount of food consumed is not large. For example, Clara has strict rules about what she can and cannot eat. Sometimes just eating one or two cookies makes Clara feel like she binged. Even though one or two cookies is a normal amount of food, Clara feels out of control while she is eating them.

What Is Your Binge Pattern Like?

To gather more information about your binge pattern, complete the following worksheet. Look at the example first.

Tracking Binges Worksheet Example

Situation	Length of Eating Episode	Food/Drink Consumed	Feelings after Eating	Objec- tively Large Binge?	Felt Loss of Control?	Type of Eating
Fight with boyfriend, felt angry and frustrated	*1 hour*	*4 rows of crackers ½ block of cheese 8 pieces of toast with butter and jam 2 large glasses of chocolate milk 3 pastries*	*Felt like I blew it again ashamed, guilty, very tired*	*Yes*	*Yes*	*objective binge*
Feeling very hungry	*15 minutes*	*1 pancake with syrup*	*Feeling very guilty, broke diet, shouldn't have eaten that*	*No*	*Yes*	*subjective binge*

Tracking Binges Worksheet

Think back over the past few weeks. Record three episodes when you felt that you had a binge. Record where you were, how you felt, or what you were doing; the length of the eating episode; exactly what you ate and drank, including the amount; how you felt afterward; whether the binge was objectively large; and whether you felt loss of control during the eating episode. In the last column determine what type of eating this is (objective binge, subjective binge, objective overeating). If you are unsure whether your binge is objectively large, try to compare it to what a typical person would eat as a meal or a snack.

Situation	Length of Eating Episode	Food/Drink Consumed	Feelings after Eating	Objec- tively Large Binge?	Felt Loss of Control?	Type of Eating

What was your *average* number of objective binges per week for the last three months? ____

What was your *average* number of subjective binges per week for the last three months? ____

Compensating Behaviors

People with bulimia use a number of methods to try to prevent weight gain after a binge, but there are two main types of compensating behaviors: purging and nonpurging.

Purging Behaviors

Purging behaviors include self-induced vomiting, misuse of laxatives, diuretics, or enemas, and the use of herbal "cleansing" remedies or "diet teas" that are usually laxative or diuretic agents in disguise. People with diabetes may misuse their insulin by not taking the proper dose or missing a dose altogether as a way of getting rid of calories. Insulin omission leads to a catabolic state, which is where muscle and fat tissue are broken down and calories are rapidly lost from the body, escaping in the urine. In the short term, this can lead to life threatening dehydration and diabetic ketoacidosis and, in the long term, damage to the eyes, kidneys, and nerves through diabetic microvascular complications. Individuals who need to take thyroid medication may take increased amounts as a way of avoiding weight gain. This can lead to menstrual irregularities, osteoporosis, heart arrythmias, and even damage to the heart muscle.

Nonpurging Behaviors

Nonpurging behaviors include excessive exercise, caloric restriction (restricting the quantity or quality of your eating), fasting (extreme caloric restriction for an extended period of time such as eight hours or more), and chewing food and spitting it out.

What is excessive exercise? Excessive exercise, also called overexercising, is associated with one or more of the following features:

* exercise is done with the sole purpose of controlling weight or weight loss

* the amount of activity is extreme

* exercise occurs despite illness or injury

* exercise is associated with a feeling of "having to" rather than "choosing to"

* exercise interferes with social activities and/or work obligations.

Calorie restriction means eating less than normal calorie levels for your age and size. The normal range that we tell clients is between 1,800 and 2,200 calories a day for women. You may restrict your calories by using diet products, eliminating certain foods, eating smaller portions, and reducing the number of meals or snacks that you have.

Other nonpurging behaviors include the use of appetite suppressants and herbal and dietary products that contain ephedrine (also called ephedra or ma huang) as an ingredient. Makers of ephedrine-containing products make health claims about their products that do not have any scientific basis (such as "lose weight while you sleep" or "burn off fat fast"). People take these products to increase their energy to exercise and to lose weight. However, ephedrine is an amphetamine-like substance that can have very harmful stimulant effects on your nervous system and heart, including increased blood pressure, rapid heart rate, nerve and muscle damage, stroke, memory loss, heart rate disturbances, seizures, heart attacks, anxiety, and psychosis, and even death (United States Department of Health and Human Services 1997). People who take ephedrine may feel revved up, jittery, anxious, and may have trouble organizing some of their thoughts.

Compensating Behavior Checklist

Review the list of compensating behaviors and check off the behaviors that you use as a way of preventing weight gain.

Purging Behaviors

_____ vomiting

_____ laxatives

_____ diuretics

_____ enemas

_____ "diet" or "cleansing" teas

_____ other (specify: _____)

Nonpurging Behaviors

_____ excessive exercise (type: _____)

_____ restricting calories (amount eaten or types of food)

_____ fasting

_____ ephedrine-containing products

_____ diet pills or other appetite suppressants

_____ chewing food and spitting it out

What was the *average* number of times that you exhibited one or more of these behaviors per week over the past three months? _____

Do You Have Bulimia?

Eating disorders can take many different forms. Some patterns have specific names (such as bulimia nervosa and anorexia nervosa), and others do not. If your binge eating and compensating behaviors occur on average at least twice a week for at least three months, then you may have bulimia nervosa. If your symptoms are less frequent, you may not meet the formal criteria for bulimia nervosa, but you may still have a serious eating disorder. We know from research that there is very little difference in symptom severity and profile between someone who binges and purges twice a week and someone who binges and purges once a week (Garfinkel et al. 1995). If you binge but do not use any compensating behaviors, or if you eat normal amounts (subjective binges) followed by compensating behaviors, you may have an eating disorder called eating disorder "not otherwise specified" (APA 2000, 594–595). This category includes people with many different combinations of symptoms. This book will be useful to anyone who struggles with the symptoms described above.

Your Self-Esteem

If you are struggling with bulimia, you probably tend to evaluate yourself based on how satisfied or, more likely, dissatisfied you are with your weight and shape. In other words, if you are feeling dissatisfied with your weight and shape, you are likely to generalize this feeling to other aspects of yourself and be dissatisfied with yourself in general (not just your weight and shape). This is true for chronic dieters, who are very concerned about their weight and shape and who experience frequent weight fluctuations as a result of trying to control their weight. In a study of chronic dieters, those who believed that they had gained weight reported that they felt less competent at work or school and less confident in their ability to interact with others (McFarlane, Polivy, and Herman 1998). This type of self-evaluation is unhealthy because it leads to very low self-esteem. In addition, low self-esteem leads to decreased socializing and impaired performance that, in turn, leads to even lower self-esteem.

When people evaluate themselves, they often base their opinion on several different aspects of themselves. One person may take pride in being a good friend, doing her best at her job, and being honest and fair in her interactions with other people, whereas another person may feel that being a good mother, an accomplished musician, and a good runner are the most important parts of herself. When a person is having trouble in one area (conflict at work, stress related to her children), she may continue to feel satisfied with other aspects of herself that she considers important (being a good friend, being honest). Although difficulty in any area may be stressful, it does not necessarily erase or undo her accomplishments and values in other areas.

When you are struggling with bulimia, however, it is common for you to believe that weight and shape are the most important aspects of yourself. You may also believe that weight and shape will influence your functioning in other areas that you consider important. For example, you may believe that you will have better relationships if you are at your preferred weight, or you may believe that nothing else matters if you weigh too much. The situation is similar to having all of your eggs in one basket and, as you will see a little later, this particular basket is full of holes.

Consider the following example. Kelly has been struggling with bulimia for four years. The pie chart below represents her entire self-esteem. Each wedge represents a different aspect of herself that she considers important. The size of each wedge represents the importance that aspect plays in her self-worth. The larger the wedge, the more important that aspect is to her self-worth (Geller, Johnston, and Madsen 1997).

Kelly's Self-Esteem Pie Chart

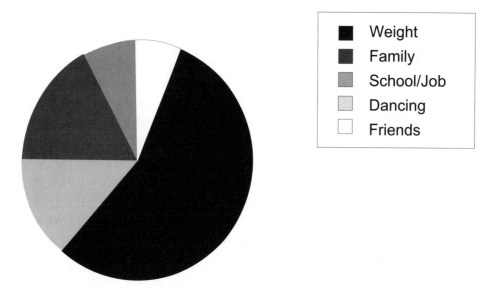

■	Weight
■	Family
■	School/Job
▢	Dancing
□	Friends

Kelly feels that her relationships with her family and her performance at school and, to a lesser extent, her ability as a dancer and her relationships with her friends are important to her self-esteem. However, it is clear that the most important domain is her weight. An important part of recovery is to shift this method of evaluating yourself and to learn to derive self-esteem from the other areas of your life, regardless of what is happening with your weight and shape. For Kelly, this does not mean that she will be able to remove weight entirely from her self-esteem pie, but rather the goal is to decrease the size of the weight wedge and place more emphasis on the other areas that she identified. Over time, it may be important to identify additional sources of self-esteem that have been crowded out or blocked by an overconcern with weight and shape.

The first step to reducing weight-related self-evaluation is to determine to what extent you engage in this type of self-evaluation. Take time to complete the following pie chart for yourself, just as you are right now. It may also be useful to complete a self-esteem pie chart to represent where you would like to be in terms of your self-esteem six months from now. Later on in this book, we will focus more directly on how to shift your self-evaluation and boost your self-esteem.

Your Self-Esteem Pie Chart

This exercise does not measure whether you have high or low self-esteem. Instead, the focus is on what is important to you when you evaluate your own self-worth. Consider all the things in your life that you are using right now to evaluate yourself as a person. Identify the different domains of your self-esteem and draw a wedge into the pie to represent each domain. Remember that the size of the wedge represents the importance of that domain when you are evaluating yourself as a person. Label your wedges.

Possible domains of self-esteem include but are not limited to . . .

- personality
- appearance
- volunteer work
- creativity
- relationships
- athletic ability

- artistic ability

- spirituality

- weight
- shape
- performance at work/school
- talents (e.g., dance, music)
- hobbies
- role as a mother/sister/partner/mentor

- competence/knowledge in certain areas

- achievements

- morals/attitudes/values (honesty, openness, speaking up, helping others, not being taken advantage of, etc.)

In six months from now, how would you like your self-esteem pie chart to look? Consider all the potential domains that you can use to evaluate yourself as a person. Identify the ones you would like to use, and draw a wedge into the pie to represent each domain. Remember that the size of the wedge represents that domain's relative importance to you. Label your wedges.

Possible domains of self-esteem include but are not limited to . . .

- personality
- appearance
- volunteer work
- creativity
- relationships
- athletic ability
- artistic ability
- spirituality
- weight
- shape
- performance at work/school
- talents (e.g., dance, music)
- hobbies
- role as a mother/sister/partner/mentor
- competence/knowledge in certain areas
- achievements
- morals/attitudes/values (honesty, openness, speaking up, helping others, not being taken advantage of, etc.)

Your self-esteem six months from now:

Consequences of Bulimia

Eating disorders are associated with the highest rate of physical and psychological complications, compared to any other psychological disorder. Bulimia has many consequences, both physical and psychological. In this section, you will learn about the consequences of bulimia and specifically about how your bulimia has affected you. We are not going over these consequences to raise your fear level. Rather, it is our goal to increase your understanding of how bulimia is affecting you both physically and emotionally. This increased awareness will help you to understand the impact the eating disorder is having on your life, as well as give you some motivation for recovery.

The important thing to know is that the majority of these physical and psychological complications are not permanent. Once you are on your way to recovery, you will start to see almost all of these complications reverse. You will start to feel better physically and emotionally. This does not mean that recovery is easy. In fact, recovery is a challenging and bumpy road and often you will feel worse before you feel better. But in the end, there is hope that you will be able to get your life back, with your physical and emotional health intact.

Physical Complications

In this section we review common physical or medical complications of bulimia based on the work of de Zwann and Mitchell (1993). As you read through each of the physical complications, you can determine the extent to which you may be experiencing these effects.

Purging Consequences

Approximately ten percent of individuals with an eating disorder will die from complications as a result of their eating disorder. Purging behaviors are dangerous because they cause fluid loss that may lead to extreme fluctuation in the body's salt levels (potassium in particular). This salt imbalance (also called an electrolyte imbalance) can lead to a heart condition called an arrhythmia that can be fatal (Pomeroy and Mitchell 2002).

If you are purging, it is important for you to have your blood checked on a regular basis for your electrolyte (salt) levels. If these levels are out of balance, your doctor may prescribe medication. Of course, to have your blood checked regularly means telling your family doctor about your eating disorder. We know that this may be very difficult to do, but it is one of the first steps to taking your health back into your own hands.

It is important to know that although people use purging behaviors as a way of preventing weight gain, not all these behaviors work in the way that they are intended. For example, laxatives get rid of water and waste from your lower intestine. By the time the food has reached this point it is fully digested and most of the calories have been absorbed. One study showed that taking very large doses of laxatives lead to wasting only twelve percent of the calories that had been eaten (Bo-Linn, Santa Ana, Morawski, and Fordtran 1983). After using laxatives, you may notice that your weight is lower—this is due to a substantial amount of fluid loss and not actual calorie loss. Because your body has lost fluid that it needs to function, it may respond by overcompensating and retaining extra water over the next few days, which causes your weight to increase until your water levels balance out. People who use laxatives may notice that their weight fluctuates quite a bit, due to this cycle of water loss and retention. In addition, since laxatives are drugs, your body builds up a tolerance over time so that you need to keep increasing the dose. You can become dependent on laxatives so that your bowel will no longer function without them. This is another risk associated with laxative use.

Similarly, vomiting does not get rid of all the calories consumed during a binge and the fluid lost during vomiting can lead to electrolyte abnormalities. Diuretics function by getting rid of fluid and not calories and, similar to laxatives, the body responds with rebound fluid retention.

Menstrual Irregularities

Chaotic eating associated with bulimia can cause irregularities in your menstrual cycle. Also, if you are vomiting and on the birth control pill, you may be vomiting your pill, and so you should use additional birth control measures.

Fatigue and Headaches

You may experience tiredness, lethargic feelings, and low energy. Frequent headaches are also a common complication. However, if you experience headaches that are very severe or different from what you are used to, you should see your family doctor.

Osteoporosis

Some people develop osteoporosis, a condition where your bones become less dense, more brittle, and therefore more prone to breaking. This is because your body needs calcium and vitamin D, which it gets from your consumption of dairy products as well as other foods. If you are severely restricting your food intake and not getting enough calcium and vitamin D, your body will start to take it from your bones.

Electrolyte Imbalance, Parasthesias, and Heart Irregularities

As mentioned earlier, fluctuations in your body's fluid levels can lead to salt imbalances of sodium and potassium called electrolyte abnormalities. These salts are important for your muscles to work properly. As your heart is a muscle, these salts are essential for your heart to beat regularly. Electrolyte imbalance can cause parasthesias—tingling feelings in your hands and around your mouth—as well as an irregular heart rhythm that, in extreme circumstances, can result in death.

Gastrointestinal Complications

Numerous stomach and intestinal complications may result from bulimia. For example, Sandy thought she had irritable bowel syndrome or possibly an ulcer. She had burning and pain in her stomach when she ate and cycles of diarrhea and constipation. She didn't tell her doctor that she was bulimic. Her doctor sent her for a full medical workup including many expensive and invasive tests (including a colonoscopy). All the tests came back normal. She was given recommendations to change her eating habits and medication for her gastrointestinal symptoms.

The symptoms that Sandy was experiencing were actually caused by her eating disorder and not a gastrointestinal condition. If Sandy had let her doctor know about her eating disorder, she could have avoided the discomfort, time, and expense of unnecessary tests and medications. She also would have been able to get more effective treatment sooner. Once Sandy did receive treatment for her eating disorder, she normalized her eating and stopped purging. Only at this point did her gastrointestinal system return to normal.

A common gastrointestinal complication of bulimia nervosa is delayed stomach emptying. This means food is staying in your stomach longer and you feel full for a long time after eating. You may also feel a lot of bloating and gas when you eat. This can be very painful. These complications result from extreme fasting or caloric restriction and are caused by your body's digestive system slowing down. Once you begin to eat more regularly and in a more normal fashion, your digestive system will speed up to normal again. However, it may feel worse before it feels better and this can make recovery a very frustrating process.

When you eat, food travels down a long tube, your esophagus, to your stomach. Your esophagus was meant to be a one-way street. Repeated vomiting turns it into a two-way street; repeated exposure to the acid from your stomach can cause tears in the lining of the esophagus and you may also see blood in your vomit. This is very serious and if you do see blood in your vomit, you should see your doctor immediately. Where the esophagus connects to the stomach, a valve opens when food comes·down and then closes to keep the contents in your stomach and prevent acid from going up into the esophagus. Repeated vomiting can loosen this valve. The consequence is a condition called reflux, where food and acid from the stomach travel back up the esophagus and into your mouth. Reflux is a condition that may or may not go away once you stop vomiting.

Repeated vomiting may also lead to swollen salivary glands. These glands are located just underneath your jaw, back towards your ears. When these glands get swollen, it may be very noticeable and your face may look larger, which can make things even more difficult when you are already struggling with body-image issues. For most people, the salivary glands return to normal size after they stop vomiting.

Kidney Complications

Purging behaviors and use of diuretics cause fluid loss that can lead to dehydration and kidney dysfunction, which is very serious and can be permanent.

Dental Problems

Cavities and erosion of the enamel on your teeth are a common consequence of bulimia. We have often been told by patients that their dentist was the first person to ask them if they had an eating disorder. Acid in your mouth from vomiting erodes your tooth enamel, leaving your teeth more vulnerable to cavities. Cavities are also increased due to binges and the consumption of large quantities of sugary foods. Unfortunately, tooth damage is permanent. It is a good idea to tell your dentist about your eating disorder so that you can receive good advice and care.

Complications from Laxative Abuse

Laxatives can cause a condition called cathartic colon where the body loses control of the bowel. Other complications include dehydration and rebound edema (swelling of the hands, legs, feet or face as your body overcompensates for water loss), electrolyte abnormalities, changes in the shape of your fingers and toes, and muscle cramping.

If you are trying to stop using laxatives, the best option is to stop them completely. If you are using mega-doses of laxatives, however, then tapering off is recommended. In any case, it is best to consult with your family doctor. Expect to have temporary water retention when you stop the laxatives. Make sure that you are taking in enough fluids so that you avoid dehydration and constipation. You should increase your intake of high fiber foods. You should also monitor the frequency of your bowel movements. If you go more than three to four days without a bowel movement, you should see your doctor. Constipation from stopping laxatives can in some cases lead to bowel obstruction. You can also use a natural fiber agent in your diet to help improve your regularity. Consult a pharmacist who will be able to give you the options for natural fiber agents. Later on in this book, we will give you some strategies to help stop using laxatives.

More Physical Complications

You may also notice that your hair, nails, and skin have become dry and unhealthy looking. As you can see from the physical consequences reviewed above, chaotic eating and purging symptoms take a toll on every aspect of your body.

Psychological Complications

The psychological complications of your eating disorder can be a direct result of the physical complications. Problems may also result from the deprivation of chronic dieting and the stress of having an eating disorder (dissatisfaction with your body shape and weight, not being able to maintain your dietary rules, feeling out of control). Each of the psychological consequences of bulimia is described in detail below. As you read through each of these consequences, you can determine the extent to which you may be experiencing these effects.

Depression

It is very common for people with bulimia to report symptoms of depression. For some people, depression preceded their eating disorder, and for others, depression developed after their eating disorder. You may notice that your mood is low and you may feel sad and unable to enjoy the things that you used to take pleasure in. You may have withdrawn from social activities. Your mood may interfere with your ability to concentrate, and you may have difficulties sleeping (not being able to fall asleep or feeling like you are sleeping all the time). You may notice a shift in your energy level such that everyday things have become momentous chores, and just getting out of bed or doing basic activities are major events. Feelings of worthlessness and hopelessness are also symptoms of depression. You may feel helpless and powerless to change your life.

Some people feel so hopeless that they have thoughts about hurting themselves or ending their life. If you are having suicidal thoughts, this is very serious and it is very important that you tell someone (a friend, family member, or doctor). If you feel that this is too difficult or that you have no one to turn to for support, you can look in your phonebook for the number of the crisis line. This number is usually listed in the front of the phonebook and the person who takes your call will be trained to provide you with the support and help that you need.

Depressive symptoms can be very serious and very upsetting to your life. The important thing to remember is that your depression will not last forever, even though it may feel that way at the time. We know from research that, with time, most depressive symptoms will improve. If your depressive symptoms began after your eating disorder, we know that these symptoms will improve once you have normalized your eating and are on your way to recovery. If your depression is severe or if you are too depressed to consider working on recovery from your eating disorder, it is important to talk to your family doctor. There are a number of medications and psychological treatments for depression that may help to alleviate your distress and suffering. In chapter 10, we will discuss the link between bulimia and depression in more detail and cover strategies to help alleviate symptoms of depression.

Anxiety

Anxiety is common in people with bulimia. You may find yourself having increased social anxiety about eating functions, social gatherings, or people noticing you or thinking negatively about you. You may have increased worries about daily activities and about the future. You may have significant anxiety about eating certain foods. You may also experience increased anxiety more generally and even panic attacks. You may also have an increase in obsessive thoughts and compulsive rituals, particularly about food. You may feel compelled to follow a rigid routine and rules about when and how you will eat. In chapter 10, we also cover different types of anxiety problems as well as strategies to help you manage symptoms of anxiety.

Mood Swings

People with bulimia often report that their mood shifts up and down. They find themselves more moody, irritable, and sensitive to comments and criticisms. This increased sensitivity also triggers mood fluctuations.

Difficulties with Concentration and Memory

Difficulties concentrating or remembering things, being easily distracted, and finding it hard to get things done or focus on conversations are common consequences of bulimia. You may find it hard to read, sit through a movie, or carry out activities necessary for work or school. When you are preoccupied with thinking about weight, shape, and food all the time, you have less mental resources available for other tasks.

Difficulties with Judgment and Decision Making

You may find it hard to make simple decisions; you may feel very indecisive and unsure. What clothes to wear, what errand to run, and what task to work on first are all small decisions that may no longer feel easy to make. These difficulties often lead to feelings of being incompetent, ineffective, and overwhelmed.

Social Isolation

Many social activities and social gatherings revolve around food. Common phrases you have probably heard include, "Why don't we go out to dinner to celebrate?" or, "Let me cheer you up—why don't we go for an ice cream?" People eat to celebrate, to reward themselves, to make things feel better emotionally, to bond with family and friends. Eating is an important part of daily life, not just in order to survive nutritionally but as a context for socializing with others. When you have bulimia, eating activities take on a whole new meaning, and rather than being fun, they may become major stressful events.

It is no surprise then that a common consequence of bulimia is for people to withdraw from social functions and from people more generally. You may not want to eat with others or be around food, and so you may miss social and family functions. You may come up with excuses as to why you can't attend a social activity, or you may cancel at the last minute. This may be about the food, or it may be that you are feeling bad about yourself and your body. People also like to dress up and look good on social occasions, and when you have bulimia, this is a challenge because you may be feeling very bad about your body and your appearance in general.

When friends or family members do not know about your eating disorder, they may get frustrated with you for making excuses and canceling events. This may lead to further withdrawal and leave you feeling socially isolated. These feelings in turn feed into the eating disorder cycle, often by fueling urges to binge, as a way to feel better or comforted, or by increasing your resolve to diet, as a way to feel more in control.

Sleep Disturbances

Another consequence of bulimia is disturbed sleep. Some people have difficulty falling asleep or staying asleep. Others find they wake up very early and cannot get back to sleep. These difficulties leave you feeling tired and lethargic throughout the day and also decrease your ability to think and concentrate.

Impulsive Behaviors

Another feature associated with bulimia is increased feelings of impulsivity. This may take the form of excessive drinking or drug use, engaging in impulsive or unprotected sex, self-harm behaviors such as cutting or skin picking, shoplifting, and engaging in other reckless behaviors without regard to safety (such as walking alone in a dangerous area at night). In chapter 9, we will discuss this topic in more detail and provide helpful strategies for managing these impulsive behaviors.

Self-Esteem Deficits

Although low self-esteem may contribute to the development of bulimia, bulimia also causes a lowering of self-esteem. When your eating is out of control, it can feel like your life is out of control too, leading to negative feelings about yourself. If you are experiencing any of the psychological complications of bulimia, you may also feel worse about yourself. You may feel worthless and have excessive guilt about things you have or haven't done. Because it is impossible to follow a diet all the time, every time you break your diet or binge and purge, you feel worse about yourself and your ability to control your eating, your weight and shape, and your life. You may find that your feelings about yourself fluctuate depending on whether you were able to follow your eating rules or whether you had symptoms. These are common feelings associated with bulimia. As you work through this book, you will learn strategies to take control back from your eating disorder and start the process of feeling better about yourself in a more stable and lasting way.

Physical and Psychological Complications Checklist

Bulimia can have a major impact on both your physical and emotional health. Check off each symptom below that you are experiencing. Some of the complications you may not be aware of unless you have had a full examination by your family doctor.

physical complications	psychological complications
____ changes to your hair, skin, and nails	____ depression
____ menstrual irregularities	____ suicidal thoughts
____ fatigue, lethargy	____ social anxiety
____ headaches	____ worrying
____ osteoporosis	____ panic attacks
____ electrolyte imbalance	____ obsessive compulsive symptoms
____ parasthesias (tingling/ numbness feelings)	____ mood swings
____ heart irregularities	____ impaired concentration and memory
____ delayed stomach emptying	____ difficulties with judgment and decision making
____ bloating, gas, and stomach pain	____ social isolation
____ blood in vomit	____ sleep disturbance
____ reflux	____ decreased self-esteem
____ swollen salivary glands	____ self-harm behaviors
____ kidney complications	____ drug use and abuse
____ dental problems	____ alcohol use and abuse
____ dehydration	____ shoplifting
____ constipation	____ excessive shopping
____ diarrhea	____ risky sexual behaviors
____ edema	
____ muscle cramps	

The Recovery Process

Recovering from bulimia nervosa is a process that takes time. There is no magic wand or magic pill that can make your eating disorder disappear. Part of the process of recovering from your eating disorder is the realization that there may be some good things about your eating disorder and some of your eating disorder symptoms. Your eating disorder may be serving an important function or coping method in your life. In fact, the conflict between the costs and benefits of your eating disorder can lead to ambivalence about recovery. One day you may want nothing more than to stop bingeing and vomiting, and the next day you may decide that you cannot cope without your eating disorder. This may make you feel like you are losing your mind or that you are not motivated to change, but the truth is that ambivalence about recovering from your eating disorder is a normal and expected part of the recovery process.

The Stages of Change

Research has shown that there are five different stages to recovering from an eating disorder. They are: precontemplation, contemplation, preparation, action, and maintenance (Prochaska and DiClemente 1982).

The first stage is referred to as the *precontemplation stage.* People who are in the precontemplation stage do not think that they have a problem. They believe that they have things under control and that they can stop whenever they want. Alternatively, they believe their eating disorder is working for them and they are not ready to even consider changing. Since you are reading this book, you are probably no longer in the precontemplation stage because it is unlikely that someone in this stage would be interested in reading a book about recovering from bulimia nervosa. If you do not think you have a problem, why would you want to change? Having said this, it is still possible for an individual in the precontemplation stage to pick up this book, as a result of pressure from friends and family or out of curiosity. If this is the case for you, it is still possible to benefit from the information in this book, either now or sometime in the future. If you are not in the precontemplation stage, you may remember a time early in your illness when you were. This may have been a time when the complications from your eating disorder were minimal or did not seem important, and restricting and purging were effective ways to feel in control or to maintain your weight.

As professionals in the field of eating disorders, we often hear, "My daughter/friend/sister/girlfriend has an eating disorder and is not interested in getting help. Every time I try to speak to her about this, she gets very defensive and angry. How can I convince her to go for treatment?" The answer is simple but not satisfying to the often desperate and worried loved one—it is not effective or even helpful to force someone to change; it is better for her to come to that decision on her own. Usually what eventually happens is that the psychological and physiological complications become too severe, too disruptive, or too costly and you move from the precontemplation stage to the *contemplation stage.*

During the contemplation stage, you will find that you are constantly weighing the pros and cons of changing or not changing. On some days, you have had enough and want nothing more than to stop your symptoms; on other days, this is too frightening or too difficult to consider. The key here is to weigh the pros and cons carefully and make a decision about whether now is the time to make a change.

Many people find it helpful to try recovery as an experiment. You already know what it is like to live with an eating disorder, and it is likely that something is not working for you, or you would not be reading this. Perhaps it is time to see what life is like without the eating disorder. This is not to say that your life will be perfect once you make changes, but it is at least worth finding out. Try recovery for twelve months, six months, or three months. Collect the data and see. If you decide you cannot cope without the eating disorder, or you cannot tolerate your body, remember that you can always go back to disordered eating.

Once you have decided to make changes, you have moved into the *preparation stage*. This means you are gathering your resources and psyching yourself up to do the hard work. The preparation stage is really a window of opportunity and people may move into the next stage of recovery (the *action stage*) or slip back into the contemplation stage. The key to moving into the action stage is to find a change strategy that will work for you.

The action stage involves using the strategies and suggestions outlined in this book. This is not an easy thing to do. This could be the most difficult thing you have ever done. As you will see in the next chapter, the eating disorder has a way of taking on a life of its own, and you may be caught up in a vicious cycle that maintains your eating disorder. In some ways you will have to draw on our expertise and trust that what we propose is an effective way to recover from your eating disorder. There is not an easier or less painful method for recovery, or we would be sharing it with you. The action stage includes normalizing your eating and using strategies to avoid acting on urges to binge, vomit, abuse laxatives, overexercise, or engage in other eating disorder symptoms.

When you have normalized your eating and, for the most part, stopped the eating disorder symptoms, you are in the *maintenance stage*. During this stage, it is likely that distressing thoughts and feelings will continue to surface, which makes sense because you will no longer be using your symptoms as a coping mechanism. Therefore the work continues. It is also important to make plans about what to do in future stressful situations to prevent symptoms, and think about what to do if urges or symptoms start to reemerge. This relapse prevention work is outlined in chapter 12.

Take a moment to consider which stage you are in: precontemplation, contemplation, preparation, action, or maintenance. Which best characterizes the stage of recovery you are in at this moment?

_____

_____

The Function of Your Eating Disorder

One of the reasons that an eating disorder can be difficult to recover from is that it may serve an important purpose in your life. Figuring out how your eating disorder symptoms benefit you is an important part of recovery. For example, for some people, restricting food and overexercising is a way to feel in control or to gain praise and attention from others. For others, bingeing or vomiting may be a way to suppress or mask difficult thoughts or feelings. In the first case, it might be necessary to find healthier ways to feel in control or to gain praise and attention, whereas in the second case it may be important to learn to identify and process the thoughts and feelings more directly.

Consider the following case. Aimee is a thirty-year-old legal secretary who has struggled with bulimia for the past twelve years. She is fed up with her eating disorder because she believes it has ruined her life. She is severely depressed, has serious difficulty concentrating at work, and, as a result, makes careless mistakes, avoids social functions, and feels she has withdrawn from most of her friends. She is chronically exhausted, her hair is thin and brittle, and her knuckles are raw from using her fingers to vomit after bingeing. Despite these serious complications, she still finds herself bingeing and vomiting every Friday and Saturday evening. At first glance, it is hard to imagine that there could be anything good about Aimee's eating disorder. But it turns out that the bingeing and vomiting have a very important function for Aimee.

When Aimee was asked about her thoughts and feelings preceding an episode of bingeing and vomiting, she reported that she is usually thinking, "I am such a loser, alone again on a Saturday night." This triggers thoughts about her desire to have a partner and also her doubts that this will ever happen. Aimee ends up feeling very sad and lonely and usually ends up in a convenience store buying food to binge on. After an episode of bingeing, Aimee no longer feels lonely or wonders about her inability to develop a significant relationship. Rather she is feeling anxious and guilty about the food she has just consumed, and is preoccupied about what it will do to her body, despite her attempt to compensate for the binge by vomiting. Although the guilt and anxiety is not pleasant, it is more manageable and less threatening than believing that she will be alone for the rest of her life.

Consider another case. Kelly is a twenty-two-year-old university student who has been restricting, bingeing, and taking laxatives for the past four years. Both Kelly and her parents have high expectations for her in terms of her future career. However, because of Kelly's eating disorder, she has been unable to graduate from university. Kelly has tried to stop her bulimic symptoms before and has been successful on two previous occasions. Unfortunately, each time when it came to making the transition back into school, she slipped back into the eating disorder. After a lot of reflection, Kelly discovered that the fear of failure is so terrifying for her that it is safer to be sick. If she is struggling with her eating disorder, then no one, including herself, expects her to graduate, or to find and succeed at some outstanding career. In other words, the illness relieves an enormous amount of pressure and gives Kelly a legitimate reason for not succeeding.

Aimee uses her eating disorder to deal with negative thoughts and feelings, whereas Kelly uses her eating disorder to protect her self-esteem and to relieve stress. These are just a few of the functions or benefits that people may obtain from their eating disorder or eating disorder symptoms. The following worksheet will help you determine yours.

Functions of Your Eating Disorder Worksheet

1. Check off any of the following roles that your eating disorder serves in your life:

    _____ helps cope with negative thoughts and feelings (depression, anxiety)

    _____ relieves or manages stress

    _____ protects your self-esteem

    _____ controls your weight

    _____ suppresses traumatic memories

    _____ helps you feel in control

    _____ helps you hold the family together

    _____ gives comfort

    _____ helps you receive attention from family members and/or friends

    _____ gives you a unique identity

    _____ gives you time for yourself

    _____ relieves boredom

    _____ helps you deal with anger by channeling emotion inward

    _____ allows you to procrastinate on overwhelming tasks

    _____ it feels familiar (companion, habit)

    _____ helps you strive for perfectionism

    _____ focuses and distracts you from more difficult issues

    _____ acts as an excuse for failed expectations

    _____ gives you discipline or punishment ("I don't deserve to eat")

    _____ gives you momentary freedom (play, escape, high, "temporary amnesia")

    _____ numbs your emotions

    _____ buffers your relationships (removes emotion)

    _____ purging allows you a perception of normalcy—allows for "normal eating"

    _____ acts as an excuse for escape from daily stresses

    _____ helps you fit ideal of society

    _____ gives you a sense of accomplishment

    _____ other function _____

    _____ other function _____

2. Examine the functions of your eating disorder that you have checked off above. In the space below, explain how your eating disorder works for you in terms of the functions you identified.

_____

_____

_____

_____

_____

_____

_____

_____

_____

3. On the scale below, rate how much you need your eating disorder to serve the purposes you identified above by placing an X on the line below.

0 percent——————————————50 percent———————————————100 percent
Do not need your   Completely need your
eating disorder at all   eating disorder to
to serve these functions   serve these functions

4. Considering the functions of your eating disorder that you have identified above, you can see that your eating disorder helps to fulfill certain needs in your life. Take some time to think about these needs. What other methods do you have of getting these needs met?

_____

_____

_____

_____

_____

_____

_____

Now that you have a better understanding of the functions of your eating disorder or eating disorder symptoms in your life, the next step is to look at the costs and benefits of your eating disorder. You can use a Decisional Balance Worksheet, adapted from Miller and Rollnick (2002), to examine the costs and benefits of maintaining your eating disorder versus the costs and benefits of recovering from your eating disorder. This exercise will help you explore your ambivalence about recovery and move you along in the process of your recovery.

Take a look at the worksheets for Aimee and Kelly, and then complete your own worksheet.

Aimee's Decisional Balance Worksheet

	Costs		Benefits	
	Short Term	**Long Term**	**Short Term**	**Long Term**
Continuing with eating disorder	—my hair is in bad shape —my body is exhausted —I cannot concentrate at work —I am unable to attend social functions —I am isolated from my friends and family —deep depression —anxiety attacks —makes me feel worthless	—may cause permanent damage to my body and mind —will probably lose my job and therefore my ability to support myself —will have to depend on my family —lose all my friends —I will be alone	—distracts me from thinking about what a loser I am —distracts me from feeling lonely and alone —prevents me from thinking about my life —gives me something to do	—life-long coping mechanism —predictable, familiar —can be comforting
Working toward recovery	—lose my coping mechanism —feel miserable —feel raw and vulnerable —have nothing to do in the evenings —have no excuse to avoid social functions	—lose my best friend: my eating disorder —will have to face myself —may get hurt	—I will not be completely absorbed by thoughts of food and eating —more available and capable of attending social gatherings —able to perform my job competently —able to save money because not buying binge food	—greater possibility of meeting someone special —healthier body and lifestyle —more content —able to obtain self-esteem from my relationships and job —more money for traveling —my life will not revolve around food and symptoms —I will be free from the eating disorder

Kelly's Decisional Balance Worksheet

	Costs		Benefits	
	Short Term	**Long Term**	**Short Term**	**Long Term**
Continuing with eating disorder	—*unable to go to school* —*upsets my family* —*laxative abuse causes serious physical pain and distress* —*passing out can be frightening* —*too weak to dance* —*no desire to hang out with friends*	—*unable to pursue a career* —*will destroy my body* —*could kill me* —*interferes with all aspects of life* —*keeps me stagnant*	—*unable to attend and finish school* —*can relax* —*no pressure* —*way to feel in control* —*allows me to be taken care of by my parents*	—*no responsibilities* —*provides a good reason why I am not a successful doctor*
Working toward recovery	—*feels awful to stop using the laxatives* —*constipation, pain, bloating* —*I will have to go back to school* —*my parents will stop catering to me*	—*I will be expected to graduate with honors* —*I will be expected to excel as a doctor* —*I will be completely stressed out* —*I may not be able to do it, and I will not have my eating disorder to blame* —*I will have to take care of myself*	—*my parents will not be so worried* —*I can attend school* —*not be preoccupied with food* —*not be dependent on laxatives* —*able to hang out with friends*	—*feel better physically not relying on laxatives* —*stop passing out* —*healthier, stronger* —*happier* —*able to dance again* —*get on with my life*

Your Decisional Balance Worksheet

	Costs		Benefits	
	Short Term	Long Term	Short Term	Long Term
Continuing with eating disorder				
Working toward recovery				

Now that you have completed your Decisional Balance Worksheet, review it for contradictory points. For example, for Kelly, being unable to attend school was both a cost and a benefit of the eating disorder. Are there any contradictions in your costs and benefits?

_____

_____

_____

When you read over the costs and benefits of your eating disorder, where does it leave you in the process of your recovery? How do the benefits of your eating disorder compare to the costs?

_____

_____

_____

_____

_____

Look at the scale below. Place an X along the line to indicate how close you are to staying with the eating disorder or to starting the process of recovery.

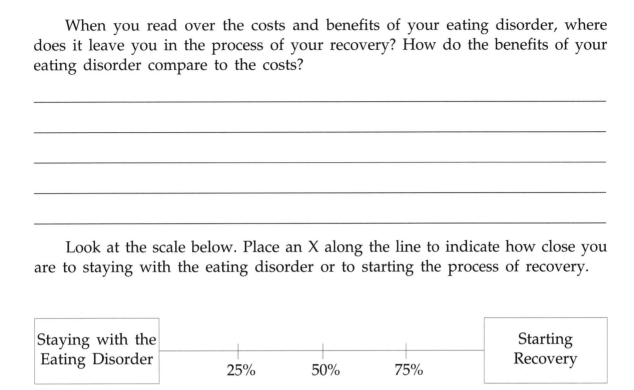

If your scale is more than 50 percent toward recovery, then you are definitely ready to try to implement the techniques described in this book. If your scale is less than 50 percent toward recovery, don't worry, that is very common. In fact, people often find that their balance shifts depending on the day and what has happened. We recommend that you read this book and try to keep an open mind. Going over the material will increase your awareness and understanding of your eating disorder, and this may help to shift your balance toward recovery and help keep it there.

Chapter 2

An Approach That Works

A model for understanding eating disorder development and recovery is illustrated in the figure below (Fairburn, Marcus, and Wilson, 1993). This model shows a pyramid divided into different tiers. An eating disorder develops from the bottom up. Low self-esteem and other underlying issues may lead you to have a negative body image and evaluate your self-worth based on weight and shape. In turn, weight-related self-evaluation can lead to attempts to change or control your body through dieting and other eating disorder compensatory behaviors such as overexercising, vomiting, and laxative use. Dieting may also lead to binge eating, and binge eating helps to maintain the compensatory behaviors.

Although an eating disorder develops from the bottom up, recovery works from the top down. Recovery begins with normalizing your eating and using strategies to control bingeing and compensatory behaviors. Once eating disorder symptoms are under control and you are working on normalized eating, the next step is to work on body image issues and weight-related self-evaluation. The final phase in recovery is to tackle self-esteem and other underlying issues that may have played a role in the development of your eating disorder.

What Causes Bulimia Nervosa?

What causes bulimia is a complicated question and will likely differ for each individual. There is no one factor or one pathway that results in bulimia; rather bulimia is a result of many factors that interact with one another. Genetic factors, messages from the media and society, individual or personality factors, early

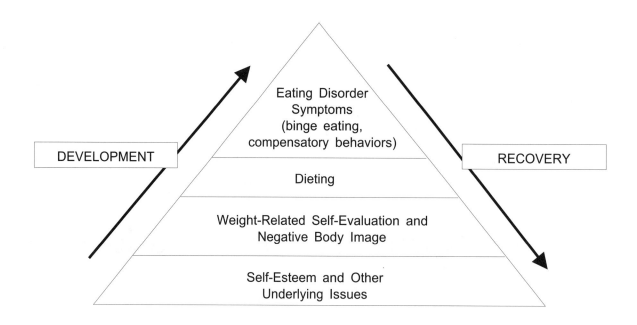

A Model for Understanding Eating Disorder Development and Recovery

experiences, and certain types of family factors can all put you at risk for an eating disorder (Garner and Garfinkel 1980). Many of these risk factors can lead to low self-esteem and encourage a connection between your self-esteem (how you feel about yourself as a person) and your weight and shape.

If your self-esteem is connected to weight and shape, and you are feeling badly about yourself, then dieting to try to alleviate the distress and increase your self-esteem seems like a logical choice. This solution is reinforced by society's message that this plan will indeed be successful. Although dieting and losing weight may make you feel better in the short term, unfortunately this will not last for long. Soon your body will adjust to the reduction in calories and your metabolism will slow down in an effort to conserve energy. When this happens, it becomes increasingly difficult to lose weight because your body is fighting against this plan and trying its hardest to maintain your weight. You may have experienced this yourself, trying to cut out even more calories or types of foods or increasing your exercise in an attempt to overcome this plateau. But your body does not like to be deprived of food, and restricting food can lead to urges to binge eat. Again, this is the body's way of trying to maintain its weight and to protect itself.

As you know, bingeing results in tremendous guilt and anxiety and serious concerns about weight gain. One way to reduce the anxiety is to try to cancel or compensate for the food you ate during the binge. This way of thinking can lead to vomiting, abusing laxatives or diuretics, overexercising, or more calorie restriction. After a while, physical and psychological complications start to surface and are exacerbated with continued symptoms. Eating disorder symptoms and the complications that result can form a vicious cycle that can keep the eating disorder alive despite efforts to change. Feeling depressed and being less able to think clearly may result from ongoing symptoms and in turn make it more difficult to think through the situation and make a change.

Risk Factors

Risk factors are events or circumstances that have been linked to an increased likelihood of having an eating disorder. Not everyone who has risk factors will develop an eating disorder and some people will develop an eating disorder without having any of these risk factors. Try to view each of the following factors as something to consider in terms of your own situation.

Biological Factors

There are a number of biological factors that may increase your vulnerability for developing an eating disorder, including your genetic makeup and body size.

Genetics. Eating disorders tend to run in families. It is not uncommon for people to report that their sister, mother, cousin, aunt, or grandmother also has an eating disorder. As in all situations of this kind, it is difficult to determine if the connection is through shared environment (such as being in a family where thinness is strongly valued) or shared genetics (biological makeup). Often it is a combination of the two. Although the exact mechanism is not clear, research suggests that eating disorders do have a genetic component (Woodside 1993). Thus, having blood relatives with an eating disorder is a risk factor.

Body size. We also know that being heavy or feeling that you are heavy is a risk factor. Being heavy or feeling that you are heavy may lead to attempts to change your body size through dieting. For example, Carol was always a heavy child. Her mother started her in an organized diet program at age nine. Carol felt that this meant she was not okay just the way she was. Over the years, Carol tried many different ways to reduce her size. She finally became successful when she developed her eating disorder.

Sociocultural Messages

It is no surprise that society seems to have a major impact on the development of eating disorders. Eating disorders are more common in societies where the media and the diet industry play a large role. You are constantly exposed to strong messages about body size and weight from magazines, commercials, television programs, films, billboards, and each other. The message is two-fold: in order to be successful, happy, worthwhile, and attractive you need to be thin; and with enough willpower, dieting, and exercise, anyone can accomplish this goal. This is absolutely not true, despite the diet industry's persistent attempts to make you believe it. The diet industry is a multi-billion dollar enterprise that makes its money based on the fact that the product that they are selling (i.e., dieting) doesn't actually work in the long run. Therefore they have a continuous stream of repeat customers willing to spend whatever it takes to find the magical method that will actually change their body.

The fact is, for some people, no matter how many sit-ups they do, they will not have the washboard stomach that is depicted in the magazines. It is physiologically not possible. Although it is unlikely that our thin-obsessed society is going to change in the near future, you can start to change how you perceive and react to these messages. One way to make a change in this area is to turn a more critical eye toward the messages and images that you are exposed to everyday. Don't just accept them at face value.

Other Risk Factors

There are a number of other risk factors that may increase your vulnerability for developing an eating disorder, including early experiences you have while growing up, family characteristics, and your personality.

Teasing. Children and adolescents who stand out in some way from others can be cruelly teased and excluded (Cash 1995). Teasing has a way of wearing away at your self-esteem, often during a critical period of development (Gleason, Alexander, and Somers 2000). Children are teased for differences in appearance, differences in sexual maturation, differences in physical or learning ability, differences in religious and cultural customs, and differences in temperament, such as being very shy or sensitive. Consider the following case. Sarah was born with a condition that left her with a facial deformity. She underwent a number of cosmetic surgeries as a child to correct the problem, but still her left eye remained deformed. She remembers vividly as a child being called "the elephant girl" and other hurtful names. She was excluded from most things on the playground and remembers spending most of her time alone dreading recess and free time. Although she had one close friend who lived next door, this friend would only hang out with her outside of school and would not allow Sarah to talk to her at school because she did not want the other kids to see them together. This made Sarah feel even worse, like there was something fundamentally wrong with her. Given that she could not change her facial deformity, she started to diet in an attempt to make herself more acceptable to herself and others.

Abuse. Sexual, physical, or emotional abuse can increase the risk of developing bulimia nervosa. This does not mean that everyone with bulimia has been abused or that everyone who has been abused has bulimia, but abuse plays a role for some individuals. Consider the following case. John is a young man who has been living with his mother and his disabled brother since his mother and father divorced, when John was three. John's mother has difficulty controlling her anger and regularly blows up at John. During these blowups, she either physically attacks John or verbally abuses him. One time, when John was fourteen, she blackened both his eyes and then threw him out of the house, telling him that he was no longer her son. John recalls incidents like this from as far back as he can remember. In addition to having a major impact on his self-esteem, this abuse was a precipitating factor in the development of his eating disorder. John started to binge and vomit in an attempt to regulate his anger and sadness related to his toxic relationship with his mother.

Lack of independence. The transition from adolescence to young adulthood is a difficult time for most people. This is when decision-making power is transferred from the parent or caregiver to the young person. For some people, the transition is drawn out for one reason or another, or there is some disagreement between the caregivers and the individual about when this transition should happen. When you are an adult and unable to make your own decisions, you can start to feel out of control, angry, or sad. This can lower your self-confidence and lead to thoughts of ineffectiveness. Believing that you are ineffective is like believing that you don't have what it takes to get the job done. Somehow, you are lacking the resources to function independently in life. These thoughts and feelings put you at risk for developing bulimia.

Malki, for example, was approaching her nineteenth birthday and was very excited about her future career as a high school teacher. She was the oldest sibling at home, in a large family of ten children being raised in an orthodox Jewish household. She was expected to follow strict rules in terms of dress, behavior, addressing and respecting her parents, household chores, and childcare. She was very bright and sociable and had a number of close friends whom she liked to spend time with. When her social life and studies started to interfere with her household duties and childcare, however, her parents responded by limiting her access to friends and deciding that she could not further her studies. She tried to reason with her parents and to explain how important her friends and her studies were to her. They did not respond, and they did not consider changing their earlier decision. Malki was left feeling sad and hopeless and felt like she didn't have a say about what happened in her life. This made her feel very badly about herself and completely out of control. One way to take charge and to feel better about herself was to control what went into her body in terms of eating or not eating. Mealtimes were a significant event in the household, and when Malki refused food this also had the added effect of enraging her parents. Despite their anger, she was able to make decisions about eating for herself, and she finally felt like she was in charge of at least one aspect of her life.

In another case, Charlene, also struggled with independence, but her problem was different from Malki's. Charlene's parents wanted "nothing but the best for her" and insisted on doing everything in their power to accomplish this. Her mother took it upon herself to do all of Charlene's shopping, laundry, cooking, and even went so far as to arrange dates for her. Her father was overinvolved in her schoolwork and actually completed all of her university applications himself.

Charlene was left feeling like she was incapable of functioning on her own and that she had absolutely no skills. This severely lowered her self-confidence and self-esteem. Charlene started to diet and exercise and initially she lost weight and toned her muscles. Friends and family commented on how good she looked and were impressed by the amount of discipline she had to make it to the gym every-day. For once in her life, Charlene felt effective, she felt like she could accomplish something and do it well.

For both Malki and Charlene, feeling out of control of their life due to family factors was a major contributor to the development of an eating disorder.

Perfectionism. Perfectionism is a personality or individual factor that increases a person's risk for developing an eating disorder. Research has shown that not only is increased perfectionism related to eating disorders (McCabe et al. 2000), it has also been linked to anxiety (Antony et al. 1998) and mood disorders (Ingram, Miranda, and Segal 1998). Although it is good to try to do your best and set goals for yourself, you can run into trouble when the standards you set are unrealistic, unachievable, and rigidly held. This type of perfectionism can play a role in both the development and maintenance of an eating disorder.

Consider the following example. Shanice was studying fashion design at school and her appearance was important not only to herself personally but also in terms of her chosen career. People in her class noticed what she wore and admired her sense of style. When she went on job interviews at upscale depart-ment stores, the impression she made on her employer was determined not only by her experience and fashion background but also by the way she looked. Shanice had always felt that she was heavier than she would like to be, and it was upsetting to her that she couldn't fit into the smaller sizes that were consid-ered "most fashionable." It was very important to her that she always look her best when she left the house, even if she was just going out to run an errand. Shanice placed a lot of pressure on herself, and it was difficult for her to relax, unwind, and just be herself. Because Shanice felt that she didn't have a "good enough" body, she also engaged in attempts to control her weight that led to the development of an eating disorder.

What Were Your Risk Factors?

As you can see, there are a variety of factors that may have placed you at increased risk for the development of an eating disorder. At this point, take some time to reflect on different influences or factors in your life that you feel may have increased your vulnerability. Use the following worksheet to outline your personal risk factors. Not only will this exercise help you to better understand how your eating disorder developed, it will also highlight underlying issues that you will likely need to tackle in later chapters.

Your Risk Factors Worksheet

For each category, think of any experiences that you have had, or factors you have had to deal with, that may have increased your risk for developing your eating disorder. Detail these factors in the space provided.

Genetic/biological risk factors (family history of eating disorders, early sexual maturation, being heavier than other children):

_____

_____

_____

_____

Sociocultural factors (media messages):

_____

_____

_____

_____

Early experiences (such as being teased):

_____

_____

_____

_____

_____

Family factors (parental expectations, importance of weight and shape in family, abuse, stressful events such as divorce, death, and so on):

_____

_____

_____

_____

_____

_____

_____

Individual factors (personality style, perfectionism):

_____

_____

_____

_____

_____

Other factors (stress, being in an environment where emphasis is placed on weight and shape such as dance, wrestling, fashion):

_____

_____

_____

_____

_____

Does Cognitive Behavioral Therapy Work?

Cognitive behavioral therapy has been the most extensively studied treatment for bulimia nervosa, and it is currently considered the standard treatment for bulimia. The research consistently shows that this treatment does indeed increase normal eating and reduce behavioral symptoms such as binge eating, vomiting, abuse of laxatives, and exercise for almost all people who continue with treatment. Also, many people who complete cognitive behavioral treatment will become completely abstinent from bulimic symptoms. In addition, there is strong evidence that beliefs and attitudes about eating and shape can also be modified with this approach (Pike, Loeb, and Vitousek 1996). Despite these promising facts about treatment, however, bulimia nervosa is known to have a relatively high relapse rate, which means that many people return to bulimic symptoms during times of stress. The high relapse rates highlight the importance of engaging in the relapse prevention work (described in chapter 12). In summary, for most people, recovery from bulimia is a realistic possibility, but the prevention of relapse may require an ongoing effort.

How to Get Started

If you have read this far, you may feel ready to begin the more active phase of recovery from bulimia nervosa. The first step is to raise your awareness by monitoring your activities, behavior, thoughts, and feelings. Self-monitoring includes keeping track of everything you eat and drink (including binges), the time and location, who you were with, urges for symptoms, actual symptoms (acting on the urge), and thoughts and feelings connected to urges and symptoms. Some people find this very hard to do because they prefer not to know what they are eating or not eating, and they feel very ashamed or embarrassed about having symptoms. You will not have to self-monitor for the rest of your life, but right now while you are focusing on your recovery, it is really important that you take the time to do it.

The purpose of self-monitoring is to help you to identify the causes of your eating disorder urges and symptoms, and also to help you to identify important targets for treatment. For example, self-monitoring helped Jenna notice that almost every time she skipped lunch, she ended up bingeing and vomiting in the evening. In another case, April realized that, more often than not, after getting off the telephone with her mother she ended up taking laxatives. Susan finally noticed that every time she stepped on a scale she ended up feeling badly and restricting her food for the rest of the day. This is the type of information that you need to know about yourself in order to effectively apply the cognitive behavioral techniques that will be described later in this book.

In addition to raising your awareness about symptoms, self-monitoring can help to keep you on track with your eating and reduce your symptoms. As you self-monitor, it is important to take note of your progress, no matter how small the change is. For some people, having breakfast on one day, or reducing bingeing and vomiting to once per day, or having a slice of pizza without vomiting, is an improvement worth noting and building on. We are not suggesting that self-monitoring is enough to cure you from your eating disorder, but we are saying that it is an important and necessary first step toward recovery.

Your Daily Journal

You may want to make a number of copies of the Daily Journal Worksheet that we've provided for you. You should make enough copies for at least two weeks. If you do not have access to a copier you can follow the daily journal format in a regular notebook. Ideally, you should use one page per day, which will allow you to review and evaluate your day more easily. If you can, you should start your record shortly after you wake up. Start with the date. Record all food and liquid that you consume. Be specific. Record both the quantity and the type of food. For example, your breakfast might include two pieces of wholewheat toast with jam and one glass of skim milk. If you are having a meal, put a bracket around it and call it breakfast, lunch, dinner, or a snack. Also, record where you are and whom you are with.

If you binge, remember to record all food and liquid that you consumed during the binge, again include quantity and type of food and put a bracket around it and label it a binge. If you have any urges to restrict your food intake, binge, vomit, take laxatives, or exercise place a "U" in the appropriate column to indicate that you have an urge for a symptom. If you act on the urge and end up restricting, bingeing, vomiting, taking laxatives, or exercising, place a check mark "✓" in the column to indicate that you have had a symptom. Finally, try to record any thoughts or feelings that you might be having, in particular if you are having urges or symptoms.

As you work on your daily journal, we don't expect you to make changes to your eating or your symptoms; you do not yet have the tools to do so. What you need is an accurate assessment of what is currently going on in terms of your eating and your symptoms.

Before you begin, take a look at the sample daily journal page from Karen's journal. You can tell a lot about Karen from looking at her worksheet. She skipped breakfast and felt good about not eating. She has made a check in the restriction column to show that she restricted breakfast. She had a restricted lunch, but had to struggle with urges to binge as her friends around her ate foods that she considers "forbidden," like French fries. After school, she cannot fight off her urge to binge any longer and goes through the drive-through of a fast food restaurant to order. She then binges in the car. Afterwards, she goes into the fast food restaurant bathroom to vomit. She feels weak, exhausted, and disappointed in herself. Back at home, she has to eat dinner with her family, so she tries to restrict the amount she has. She also restricts fats by having her potato plain. She is feeling guilty about eating anything at all. After dinner, she declines an invitation from a friend to go out, and instead she goes to the gym where she does a two-hour intense workout. Back at home, she has a green tea and bowl of pretzels before bed. She is feeling better about herself after working out. She is too tired to focus on her school assignments and goes to bed. This example illustrates how useful the daily journal can be in identifying patterns and links between eating, thoughts, feelings, and behavior. We can see that there is a connection between Karen's extreme calorie restriction and her bingeing. We can also see that what she eats plays a major role in how she feels about herself. We can see that she is struggling to control her eating, and she is also choosing to exercise rather than socialize. It is difficult for her to focus on school because she is having difficulty concentrating, due to fatigue and her preoccupation with eating and her weight. We can see that her eating disorder really seems to be affecting a number of areas of her life: how she feels, her ability to concentrate, and her social life.

Karen's Daily Journal

Date: *May 5*

Time	Food and Liquid Consumed	People Place	Restrict U=Urge ✓=Acted	Binge U=Urge ✓=Acted	Vomit or Laxative U=Urge ✓=Acted	Exercise U=Urge ✓=Acted	Thoughts and Feelings
7:00 a.m.	*Breakfast 1 cup of black coffee*	*Home*	✓				*feel good, strong*
noon	*Lunch large glass of water small bowl of steamed rice with vegetables*	*cafeteria at school*	✓	U			*feeling very hungry, difficult to concentrate on work, strong urge to order fries like friends are having, strong urge to binge*
4:00 p.m.	*Binge 2 burgers 2 large fries 2 large sodas 3 apple pies hot fudge sundae*	*after school, in car*		✓	✓		*feeling out of control, feeling good, a release, during the binge but now feel guilty and horrible, vomited in washroom, feel tired, weak*
6:00 p.m.	*Dinner 1 small piece of chicken ½ baked potato, plain cup of green beans*	*dinner with family*	✓			U	*feeling guilty for eating at all, feeling disgusted with self*
9:00 p.m.	*Snack green tea small bowl of pretzels*	*After two hour workout at gym, at home*	✓			✓	*feeling exhausted and hungry, but feel good that I worked out*

Complete your daily journal record after each meal, urge, or symptom (if necessary, be sure to take some time at the end of the day to complete the daily journal for the day). Record for at least two weeks to get an accurate baseline.

Daily Journal

Date: _____

Time	Food and Liquid Consumed	People Place	Restrict U=Urge ✓=Acted	Binge U=Urge ✓=Acted	Vomit or Laxatives U=Urge ✓=Acted	Exercise U=Urge ✓=Acted	Thoughts and Feelings

Reviewing Your Self-Monitoring

Now that you have completed two weeks of monitoring, take some time to look over your completed daily journals. Answer the following questions in the space provided. This information will be useful as you work through the next few chapters.

Do you notice any patterns?

_____

_____

_____

_____

Do you notice connections between your eating, your thoughts, your feelings, and your behaviors?

_____

_____

_____

_____

Is there a pattern with your eating disorder symptoms?

_____

_____

_____

Do you alternate between restricting what you eat and bingeing later on?

_____

_____

_____

_____

Are there connections between certain triggers and symptoms?

_____

_____

_____

Are there times in the day or days of the week when your symptoms are more likely to occur?

_____

_____

_____

_____

What areas of your life are being affected by your eating and symptoms?

_____

_____

_____

_____

Chapter 3

Regulating Your
Body Weight

This chapter and the next will cover a number of important topics that may be difficult for you at first. Some of the information about food consumption and body weight may run counter to the beliefs that you have organized your life around and have held for many years. Right now it's important to keep an open mind. Read the information in the chapters, and try to consider it as an alternative way of thinking about weight and eating. We know that it is not the only way to think about these topics and that there is plenty of information and evidence to the contrary, but we also know that this new information can provide you with a rationale and the motivation to try things differently, and it can help you to recover from bulimia.

Set Point Theory

The average height for North American women is somewhere around five feet four inches. Certainly some women are shorter than the average height and some women are taller than the average height. Height is mostly determined by genetic factors, and for the most part, you cannot successfully manipulate your height. No one seems to dispute these facts.

The same is true for weight. Some people's weight corresponds naturally to the average weight, some people's weight is naturally below the average weight, and some people's weight is naturally above the average weight. This natural weight is where your body functions best, and is the weight that your body is meant to be according to your genetic makeup (Keesey 1993). Just as you have a predetermined height or shoe size, you also have a predetermined biological weight or set point that your body tries to defend (Bennett and Gurin 1982). This set point will fluctuate by five to ten pounds in most people, and really should be viewed as a range, rather than one specific number. Your set point is determined by biological factors, including heredity and your metabolism.

Your basal metabolic rate is the amount of energy (calories) that your body requires in order to carry out your basic bodily functions such as breathing, cell regeneration, and digestion. In normal eaters (people who don't diet or have an eating disorder), the basal metabolic rate usually accounts for about two-thirds of the body's total energy needs, with the remainder being used during physical activity. Your basal metabolic rate helps to defend your set point. The way this works is as follows: If you eat more calories than is necessary to maintain your weight for a period of time, then typically your body temperature rises and your basal metabolism speeds up and burns off the excess calories. This is called diet-induced thermogenesis (Rothwell and Stock 1979). On the other hand, if you eat less than is necessary to maintain your weight, then your basal metabolism slows down to spare the available calories. This is why, for the most part, people who are normal eaters usually maintain a stable weight over time. During times of festivity, they may gain some weight due to excess eating, or during times of illness they may lose some weight due to insufficient eating, but they will usually remain within their set point range. The set point theory makes sense from an evolutionary perspective; the human race would likely not have survived during times of famine if there were not an internal mechanism for maintaining weight.

Your Set Point

By now you are probably wondering what your set point is. The only way to know for sure is to recover from bulimia and eat normally for a significant amount of time, usually one year. If you do this, then your body will migrate to its natural weight in order to run your body's vital functions to the best of its ability. Easier said than done, right? We know that most people who are recovering from bulimia want to know what they are getting themselves into before they begin. Unfortunately there is no way to know for sure. You may be able to look toward the weight of other family members as an indicator of your own set point, but remember that this is only true if your family members are normal eaters (no dieting or overeating). You may have had a time in your adult life when you were eating normally without symptoms. Your weight during this time can be indicative of your set point. Otherwise, you will need to wait and see what happens to your weight during recovery, which can be very stressful and upsetting.

There is a tendency to believe that if you eat a normal amount of food, your weight will go up and up and up, and never stop. This does not happen, but you need patience and coping strategies to find out where your weight will settle. Although your set point may be a higher weight than you would like, it is important to get accurate information about your weight, rather than assuming that it will continue to increase.

Why Dieting Doesn't Work

Natural weight can range from being very light to being very heavy. Unfortunately, for the individuals who are above average weight or even around average weight, their body does not match the thin body idealized and encouraged by society. It is these people who are most likely to try to change their natural weight by dieting. Body image dissatisfaction and dieting is prevalent in this society, and many people spend their life trying to change their weight to no avail. The literature shows that the majority of diets do not work to maintain long-term weight loss (Garner and Wooley 1991). Set point theory offers one explanation as to why most diets don't work: Caloric restriction eventually causes your metabolism to decrease and your body to use calories more efficiently, which prevents weight loss.

Dieting and Bingeing

One way you can be vulnerable to bingeing is by going on a diet and restricting your eating. Consider the following case. Susan usually tries to stick closely to a very low calorie diet of fruits and vegetables with some low fat protein such as fish or chicken. On a typical day, she wakes up and has a black coffee and a piece of fruit, usually an apple or a pear. Around lunchtime she has a salad with low fat dressing and a glass of water. On this particular day, she was invited to a dinner party to celebrate the birthday of a close friend. She ate a plate of pasta for dinner, and after considerable pressure from the host agreed to have a piece of birthday cake. Susan described feeling very much out of control after eating the birthday cake. Susan believed that she had ruined her day and that she had sabotaged her diet beyond repair. These distressing thoughts and feelings continued long after the party, and when she arrived home she had strong urges to binge and ate a whole container of ice cream and a large bag of pretzels. Why not? She believed that she had failed miserably at her diet today, and that she could get back on track with her diet tomorrow morning. Researchers Janet Polivy and Peter Herman call this experience the "what the hell" effect (1984, p.151). Sound familiar?

Overeating may be the result of eating a forbidden food (Herman and Mack 1975), but research with chronic dieters (restrained eaters) has shown that a number of different conditions can cause dieters to overeat. This includes being exposed to elevated levels of anxiety (Polivy, Herman, and McFarlane 1994), clinical depression (Polivy and Herman 1976a), feeling down (Ruderman 1985), alcohol use (Polivy and Herman 1976b), reduced self-awareness (Polivy et al. 1987), perceived weight gain (McFarlane, Polivy, and Herman 1998), and increased negative view of the self (Heatherton, Striepe, and Wittenberg 1998). The eating behavior of chronic dieters is also sensitive to the social situation the dieters are in. For example, restrained eaters will eat less in front of others and then overeat when alone (Herman, Polivy, and Silver 1979). Overeating is also triggered when the dieter has agreed to start a diet the next day (Urbszat, Herman, and Polivy 2002) or by the presence of another person who "breaks" their diet (Polivy et al. 1979).

Dieting and Weight Gain

Unfortunately, alternating between restricting and feasting is a good way to gain weight. During dieting, your metabolism slows down considerably in an attempt to spare calories. During this time, your body does the same work, but uses fewer calories. If this period of restriction is followed by a large consumption of calories, your body is primed to use the calories efficiently and save as many as possible to store as fat. For most people, this results in weight gain; it is the result of the body's adaptive mechanism of preparing for the next famine or diet. This is why people who engage in yo-yo dieting often end up weighing more than they did when they started to diet.

To reiterate, in the long run, diets don't work and, in fact, are likely to support weight gain and in some cases increase people's set point weight. Ideally, you can use this information to give up dieting and try to normalize your eating. We will talk more about normal eating in the next chapter.

Your Reaction

We understand that this information likely goes against everything that you have believed in, and may make you seriously question some of your past decisions regarding dieting and your eating disorder. Take time now to reflect on this information about set point, metabolism, dieting and weight gain, and write about your reaction. Try to identify your thoughts and how you are feeling.

_____

_____

_____

_____

_____

_____

You may feel relieved because now you have a good reason to give up the dieting once and for all. You may feel sad, frustrated, or angry about the time, energy, and money that you have spent on dieting, only to find out that it might have backfired and increased your set point. We also understand that you may not believe what we are saying at all, and that's okay. If this last option is true for you, then this is probably a good time to remind you to keep an open mind, and to at least consider other ways of thinking, all in an effort to support your recovery from bulimia.

Keys' Study of Starvation

Keys' study of starvation demonstrates the link between restriction and bingeing and also provides evidence for set point theory (Keys et al. 1950).

Ancel Keys was a professor at the University of Minnesota during World War II. This was a time of serious food shortages, and many people around the world were seriously underweight and starving. Professor Keys was interested in finding out what would be the best way to refeed starved individuals after the war. Thirty-six healthy young men agreed to participate in the study. During the study, the men were asked to move into the dormitories at the University of Minnesota and follow a semi-starvation diet for six months in order to lose 25 percent of their body weight. This was followed by three months of rehabilitation, during which the men were gradually refed. During the starvation phase, Professor Keys and his colleagues started to notice that some very strange things were happening to these men, and he started to document these experiences.

Changes in Eating Attitudes and Behavior

Like many people who struggle with an eating disorder, the men became completely preoccupied with food and eating. They spent a large amount of their day thinking about their meals and planning how they would eat them once they arrived. Once the food arrived, the men would eat in total silence and devote their entire attention to the food and eating. The men had difficulty focusing on daily activities because they were totally consumed with thoughts of food and eating. For some, the preoccupation was so intense that they even changed careers once the study was over: three became chefs and one became involved in agriculture. Interestingly, gum chewing and the consumption of tea and coffee became so excessive that these substances had to be limited by the researchers. (Many of our patients with bulimia also overuse fluids and gum, and although the exact purpose differs depending on the individual, many tell us that it is a way to avoid eating or a method to cope with hunger.)

Bulimia Cases

The men in the Keys study were free to come and go, and many of them attended classes and worked off campus. Before they began the diet, the men agreed that they would take responsibility to follow the diet and not eat any other foods. What the researchers didn't count on was that all of the men would report intense hunger, and for some, the hunger became intolerable and led to strong urges to binge eat. It became clear that the honor system would not be enough to avoid acting on the urges to eat. The men, of course, were very committed to the study and wanted to comply with the conditions. To increase compliance, they instituted a buddy system that encouraged the men to take another study participant with them when venturing off campus. Guess what? Even this did not work. A number of the men did indeed binge eat. One man, while working in a grocery store, ate several cookies, a sack of popcorn, and two overripe bananas. This man reported feeling very anxious, guilty, and disgusted with himself. He was so upset, he ended up vomiting as a way to compensate for his indulgence.

For some of the men, the binge urges and eating did not begin until the refeeding phase of the study. In other words, they were able to avoid eating until they were given permission to eat. But once the restrictions were removed, urges to binge became very difficult to avoid.

Psychological and Emotional Responses

Psychological responses to starvation observed in the men included impaired concentration, judgment, and memory, loss of interest and motivation to engage in activities previously enjoyed, including both social and sexual interactions, depression, mood swings, irritability, outbursts of anger, anxiety, apathy regarding personal hygiene, and sleep disturbances. As the study continued, many of the men began biting their nails or smoking because they felt nervous. At least three of the men actually had such a severe emotional reaction that they had to be excused from the study. One man became suicidal, another chopped off three fingers of one hand in response to stress, and another developed compulsive behaviors that included rooting through garbage cans for food.

What is most remarkable about these findings is the fact that all of the men involved in the study underwent a series of psychological tests, and all were deemed to be on the healthier end of normal before starting the study. The men's personality adjustment before starvation did not predict their emotional response to caloric restriction. In fact, some of the men who appeared to be the most psychologically adjusted reacted most severely to the starvation diet.

Physical Responses to Starvation

Physical responses to starvation observed in the men who participated in the Keys study included gastrointestinal discomfort, constipation, dizziness, headaches, hypersensitivity to noise and light, poor motor control, cardiac changes, thinning of scalp hair, dehydration, and muscular weakness. Various changes also reflected an overall slowing of the body's metabolic rate, such as significant reductions in body temperature, heart rate, and respiration.

Evidence for Set Point

There are two pieces of information from the Keys study that support set point theory. First of all, although the men all agreed to lose 25 percent of their body weight, not all of them could do this. For some men, no matter how much their actual food intake was reduced, their body kept adjusting in order to spare and store calories. Their metabolism had dropped by about 40 percent to support the body's goal of weight maintenance, which was contrary to the goal of the researchers. Finally the researchers gave up on insisting that everyone in the study lose 25 percent of their body weight. It was as if they realized that the body's natural defenses against weight loss and defending its set point were a force not to further contend with.

The second piece of evidence for set point theory comes from the rehabilitation phase of this study. Once the men were allowed to eat again, they initially gained weight very rapidly, and after eight months their weights were above their original weight. This makes sense because many of the men were still overeating in response to the deprivation they experienced in the study. However, after fourteen months, most of the participants who were eating normally returned to within a few pounds of their original weight, suggesting that eventually the body adjusts and returns to its set point.

Sims' Study of Overeating

In response to the Keys findings, another group of researchers were interested in studying the effects of overeating and weight gain (Sims et al. 1968). As you can expect, it was very difficult to find people to agree to participate in this study, so the researchers decided to use a prison population. The prisoners were given many perks including delicious food if they agreed to be in this study. (By today's standards, this type of recruitment is seen as unethical and is no longer allowed.) The prisoners agreed to gain 20 percent to 25 percent of their body weight and doubled their food intake for six months. Most of the men gained weight initially, but soon their bodies resisted further weight gain, despite continued overeating. One man stopped gaining weight even though he was eating 10,000 calories per day. The men's metabolisms had increased significantly in response to the extra calories, and they were burning off the excess energy by increased body temperature and excessive perspiring. The overeating became increasingly unpleasant, their psychological state was failing, and some men became physically ill after meals. Many of the men thought about withdrawing from the study (Sims 1976).

Evidence for Set Point

Parallel to the Keys study, there are two pieces of evidence that we can obtain from the Sims study to support set point theory. To begin with, just as the body resists weight loss, the body also makes metabolic adjustments to resist weight gain. Despite continued overfeeding, not all men were able to gain 20 percent of their body weight as planned. Their metabolisms increased in response to extra calories and burned off the excess calories to defend their bodies' set point weight.

Secondly, as soon as overeating was no longer required, most of the men rapidly lost weight and stabilized at their preexperiment weight. The only exceptions were the two men who initially gained weight very rapidly, as well as two others with a family history of obesity and diabetes. In other words, except for those who seemed to be genetically predisposed to weigh more, all men returned to their original weight or their set point.

How Does This Apply to You?

You may be wondering how the experiences of starved or stuffed men apply to you and your recovery. Given that you are not constantly in a starved state and/or you are not seriously underweight, you may think that the Keys study results do not apply to you. But remember, if you have been successful at driving your body below your set point weight, then these experiences could apply to you, despite your weight. Also, even if you are at or above your set point weight, you may be suffering from the effects of starvation. As you know, bulimia includes alternating between, on the one hand, binge eating and restricting and, on the other, general chaos with respect to eating and symptoms. It is likely that you are experiencing some of the side effects of starvation, regardless of your weight, due to the periods of restriction that are part of your bulimia.

Whether it is fasting, purging, skipping meals, or cutting back on certain food groups or calories, it is likely that your body is malnourished and experiencing temporary periods of starvation. You are also likely experiencing the effects of psychological deprivation. On the other hand, if you have binged your weight above your set point, the Sims study indicates that if you learn to eat normally and stop bingeing, your weight will likely return to a lower weight.

The message here is that many of the physical and psychological problems that you are currently experiencing are part and parcel of not eating well, and in order to make the first step toward recovery and rule out physiological urges to binge, you need to start eating normally. It is only after the effects of starvation and bingeing have been removed that underlying issues can be accurately addressed. Normalizing your eating not only stabilizes you physically and emotionally, but relief from the preoccupation with food frees up mental energy to deal with the issues underlying your bulimia. In the next chapter, we will go over the steps involved in developing a healthy relationship with food.

Taking Control of Yourself

There are a number of reasons to give up dieting and make the switch from trying to control your weight to taking control of your self and your life. Here's a reminder.

* Dieting does not lead to long-term permanent weight loss.

* Dieting lowers your metabolic rate and can lead to weight gain and increased set point weight in the long run.

* Dieting leads to many negative physical effects.

* Dieting causes a range of negative psychological consequences, including increased depression, stress, anxiety, food preoccupation, and decreased self-esteem.

* Dieting can lead to binge eating or overeating.

* Dieting leads to feelings of failure (when the diet fails) and feeling out of control (when your dietary rules are broken).

* Normalized eating leads to increased time and energy to devote to other things that are important in your life.

Chapter 4

What Is Normal Eating?

Normalized eating is quite simple. It involves having at least three well-balanced meals and possibly several snacks per day, generally around 1,800 to 2,200 calories per day for the average woman and 2,200 to 2,800 calories per day for the average man. If you are eating much less than this amount, your portion sizes are likely too small or you are consuming diet products. If you are eating much more than this amount, you are likely overeating or bingeing. Of course, this daily amount will vary slightly depending on your age and size.

Normalized eating involves eating like a person without an eating disorder, that is as a *non-dieter*. This means allowing yourself to eat normal portions from all of the food groups. Most of the time, non-dieters eat when they are hungry and stop eating when they are full. Although their eating is influenced by emotional factors, their food intake is largely controlled by the physical cues of hunger and satiety. For you, however, it is likely that your hunger and satiety cues have been disrupted by your attempts to control what you eat. So although the long-term goal is for your eating to be regulated by your internal cues of hunger and satiety, in the short term, the goal will be to schedule your eating. Scheduling your eating at proper intervals will retrain your body's internal cues, and over time, perhaps up to a year, you will notice that you are more aware of your internal signals for eating. Eating according to a schedule is a strategy called mechanical eating.

Strategies for Normalizing Your Eating

Coping strategies form the essential foundation for recovery from an eating disorder. In this book you will learn about a range of different strategies for dealing with different symptoms. This next section reviews coping strategies for dealing with restriction of your eating. The purpose of using these strategies is to help you to normalize your eating, which will also help reduce urges to binge.

Mechanical Eating

Mechanical eating involves following a schedule of eating, regardless of how you are feeling, what you are thinking, or what you are doing. This means eating breakfast shortly after you get up in the morning, lunch around noontime, and dinner in the early evening. You may also schedule snacks, if you prefer to have smaller meals and to eat more frequently. Snacks should be eaten mid-morning, mid-afternoon, and before bedtime. Mechanical eating involves planning:

1. timing of your meals (breakfast, lunch, dinner) and snacks (if you are having them)

2. what you will eat

3. where you will eat and with whom

Mechanical eating may involve eating more or less than you feel like eating at a specific time, especially in the beginning. The goal of mechanical eating is to protect you from undereating or overeating in a given situation.

To plan your eating schedule, you need to write it down in advance. You may want to plan meals each evening for the next day. Although this task may seem tiresome, it is the foundation for your recovery. Once your eating becomes more normalized, you will feel better both physically (you'll have more energy, decreased urges to binge) and emotionally (decreased anxiety and stress). Remember, you will not have to plan your meals every day for the rest of your life. Rather, this is a necessary step in the short term as you move towards recovery.

Normalized Eating As an Experiment

It is easy for us to tell you to give up dieting and try the normalized eating approach. For you, this idea may be completely scary. You may fear that if you try normalizing your eating, your weight will start to go up, and keep going up until it is out of control. Here is where you need to have faith that your weight will settle out where your body wants it to be (at your body's set point weight). Think of normalized eating as an experiment. This is something you can try for a defined period of time, such as one month, three months, six months, or one year. You can always go back to your eating disorder if you choose. What do you have to lose? This is an experiment to see what life can be like without your eating disorder. Complete the contract below to start on your experiment with normalized eating.

Normalized Eating Experiment Contract

I agree to try normalizing my eating for an experimental period of _____ .

Start date: _____

End date: _____

Food As Medicine

Another helpful strategy is to think of your meal plan and the food you eat as medicine. It is your anti-binge remedy. If you had a throat infection and your doctor prescribed you an antibiotic and told you to take it three times a day, you would not question this but would take your medicine as recommended. In the same way, a minimum of three meals is your medicine. Although you may not like doing it, in the long run, it is what you need. You can repeat this statement to yourself as you eat according to the scheduled plan: "Food is my medicine."

Eating As a Non-Dieter

You may be thinking, "I don't know how to eat like a non-dieter." Well, that is what we will teach you. A meal or snack that is non-dieting should not look diet-like to an outside observer. For example, Cleo had five celery sticks as a snack. To an outside observer, Cleo's snack seems like a diet snack. If she had added a yogurt and an apple or peanut butter with crackers, her snack would look more like a normalized snack. Alternatively, Jill had three pieces of ice cream cake for a snack. Although this is not a diet-like snack, it is not normalized eating either. Most non-dieters would choose one piece of ice cream cake. It can be helpful to look at the recommended serving size available on most packages to determine what a non-dieting meal or snack portion would be. Alternatively, you can model your serving sizes after someone you know who is a normal eater.

Eliminating diet products from your meal plan plays a central role in becoming a non-dieter. There are a number of reasons to do this. First, the majority of diet products don't taste good anyway, and people generally end up eating more of the diet product than they would have eaten of the non-dieting version of the food. Second, diet products are often gimmicks that play on your insecurity. Third, diet products in your refrigerator can serve as triggers for symptoms (increasing urges to restrict, increasing weight and shape preoccupation). Finally, eliminating diet products is part of a broader goal of working toward a non-dieting philosophy; since you are not a dieter, you do not need diet products. If your refrigerator is full of diet products, you may want to start by making a commitment not to buy anymore.

Incorporating Risky Foods

Normalized eating also involves gradually including what you consider to be risky foods, foods that you have been avoiding, or foods that you are afraid of, that you believe are fattening or believe may trigger a binge. You may avoid so-called junk foods, such as chocolate, French fries, potato chips, or ice cream. Why should you incorporate risky foods in your eating plan, you may ask? First, if you restrict these foods from your eating, it is more likely that you will binge or overeat on them later when you have broken your eating rules. It makes more sense to incorporate a normal serving in a planned way than to feel out of control and eat several servings during a binge. Second, these types of food can make you feel good. You eat them during celebrations, at parties, and for fun. So restricting these foods from your eating plan contributes to feelings of psychological deprivation. Third, restricting these foods may make it difficult for you to attend outings or social events that involve food. For example, it is hard to go to a birthday party and decline a piece of cake. Finally, from our perspective, there is no such thing as "junk food." Rather, food is just energy. It all gets broken down into the same components and is used by your body for fuel. Complete the next worksheet to identify areas to work on when you are normalizing your eating.

Your Safe Foods–Risky Foods Worksheet

Safe foods are the foods that you associate with weight loss. These are foods that are typically low in fat and are generally considered diet foods. Safe foods are usually eaten without feeling guilty or anxious and are generally viewed as "good" foods. Examine your daily journals you did in chapter 2. List your safe foods below.

_____   _____

_____   _____

_____   _____

Risky foods are the foods that you associate with weight gain. These are foods that are typically higher in fat and are often considered junk foods. Consumption of risky foods is usually associated with feelings of guilt and loss of control. List your risky foods below.

_____   _____

_____   _____

_____   _____

Guidelines for Eating Risky Foods

Using the information on your Safe Foods–Risky Foods Worksheet, follow the guidelines below for incorporating risky foods in your meal plan.

1. Incorporate risky foods into your meal plan in a gradual and planned way. Start with a food that is risky, but not the *most* risky or frightening for you. When you make gradual changes, your anxiety may increase, but over time, as you maintain the changes, your anxiety will decrease.

2. Choose a safe place. This may be a public place (a park or coffee shop with a supportive friend) where you will not be able to consume more than you planned to or get rid of what you have eaten through purging. You will want to make sure there is no extra food around that could lead to a binge. It is a good idea to choose a place where access to washrooms is limited or scarce if vomiting is a symptom for you.

3. Choose a safe time. You may want to eat the risky food earlier in the day rather than at the end of day, when you may be tired and more vulnerable to having symptoms.

4. Make sure that only one normal serving of the risky food is available. For example, buy a small bag of chips or buy an individually packaged portion of cookies. This is easier than trying to eat a normal serving from a family-size package.

5. Have an activity planned for when you finished. This will help to prevent symptoms afterwards. For example, meet a friend, leave the house, or do something fun.

6. Plan ahead!

No Good or Bad Foods

Most people with bulimia think of foods as good or bad, safe or fattening. This type of black-and-white thinking sets you up for symptoms. For example, Jessica went to a movie with her boyfriend. She hadn't eaten all day. She had restricted because she wasn't feeling very good about herself, and restricting made her feel more in control. At the movie, her boyfriend came back from the snack bar with popcorn and nachos and cheese. By this point, she couldn't resist her hunger and ate the nachos and cheese. The next day she felt even worse about herself because of what she had eaten. For Jessica, having the nachos and cheese at the movies was a lapse in control because she ate a "fattening" forbidden food. This fueled her desire to continue restricting her eating, and thus the cycle of symptoms continued.

In therapy, we worked on Jessica's interpretation of nachos and cheese as a "bad" food. Her interpretation of what she ate was the key to her feelings of guilt, shame, and the view that she was somehow weak.

If you ask non-dieters what their opinion is on nachos and cheese, many would say it is a yummy snack food. You can use this strategy to help you start to identify and shift your thinking about food. You can ask yourself: "What would a non-dieter think about this situation?" It is also helpful to think of food as just food. There are no good or bad foods. All food gets broken down to the same basic nutritional building blocks.

Three Nutritional Building Blocks

When you are planning your meals in a non-dieting way, you want to make sure that you are covering all of your nutritional needs. There are three basic sources of energy.

Carbohydrates. Carbohydrates include sugars (fruit, jam, candy) and starches (bread, potatoes, cereal, vegetables). They provide a quick source of energy and help to decrease urges to binge.

Proteins. Proteins include animal proteins (dairy products, meat, eggs) and plant proteins (nuts, beans, whole grains). Protein performs many vital roles in your body, helping to build its structural components (internal organs, muscles, hormones, blood), as well as maintain and repair muscle and tissue. Because protein is so important to your bodily functions, it is used only as a last resort when you need energy. Your body prefers to obtain energy from carbohydrates and fat.

Satiety Nutrient (Fat). Satiety nutrients include added fats (oil, margarine, butter) and fats that are already in food (chocolate, baked goods, cheese, nuts, meat). Given that fat is usually associated with a range of negative meanings, we find it helpful to relabel fats as *satiety nutrients*, focusing on their very important functioning in your eating plan. Satiety nutrient is a very concentrated form of energy that gives your body longer lasting energy than carbohydrates because it is digested more slowly. Satiety nutrients in food also keep you more satisfied and full between meals, which will decrease your preoccupation with food and urges to binge. Satiety nutrient performs vital functions in your body, such as helping fat soluble vitamins to be absorbed, protecting organs, and forming cell membranes.

The important thing to remember is that your body does not see any of these sources of energy as good or bad. Rather, they are all sources of fuel. Each fuel source has different functions in your body, but in the end, they all function to provide energy. Whether you have 200 calories of spinach or 200 calories of chocolate, your body gets 200 calories of energy. Although your body needs a variety of foods to perform its functions, there is really no such thing as a bad energy source.

A helpful guide for eating like a non-dieter is the food pyramid guide published by the United States Department of Agriculture (USDA) Center for Nutrition Policy (Welsh, Davis, and Shaw 1993). The food pyramid guide is a research-based guideline that provides a good overview of the different food groups and appropriate daily amounts. You can access this guide online at: http://www.pueblo.gsa.gov/cic_text/food/food-pyramid/main.htm

Another valuable food guide is the Health Canada food guide, which can also be accessed online at: http://www.hc-sc.gc.ca/hppb/nutrition/pube/foodguid/

Developing an Action Plan

Normalized eating is not easy work, and it doesn't happen overnight, so don't be too hard on yourself. It is better to make small changes at a gradual pace so that you can keep going forward. If recovery is your top priority, then normal eating is your top priority. This means that you need to make sure you have the planned food at the planned time. This requires planning for grocery shopping. You also need to make yourself available to do the planned eating at the planned time.

For example, when Jessica looked at her food diary, she identified breakfast as the meal she wanted to work on. She usually skipped breakfast because she was rushing to work. When she skipped breakfast, she was also more vulnerable to restricting her lunch. We brainstormed, and Jessica came up with some strategies to ensure that she had breakfast each day. For her, this meant on days she started work later, she would have breakfast at home. On days that she started work very early, she planned ahead and had cereal and milk stored in the refrigerator at work so that she could eat when she got there. This strategy worked for her. Each person is different and you will need to make the plan and think of the strategy that will work for you. Follow these steps to normalizing your eating:

1. **Plan your eating in advance.** Schedule in advance what your eating plan will be for the week. Although things may come up and you will have to improvise in some situations, having the main plan in advance will help you to do mechanical eating. Use the meal planning worksheets provided at the end of this section, or you can use your own journal. If you use the worksheets, it is a good idea to make enough copies to plan your eating for several weeks or months, depending on the length of the normalized eating experiment you have committed to. Record the times you will eat, what you will eat, and the amounts. Examples are also provided.

2. **Self-monitor your eating.** Use the daily journal format supplied in chapter 2.

3. **Review your monitoring.** After a week, sit down and review your eating pattern. Ask yourself the following questions:

   ✳ Do I have enough meals and snacks?

* How many of my meals/snacks are "dieting"?

* How is the timing of my meals/snacks?

* Am I having variety in my food choices?

* How are my portions? Are they normalized, or non-dieting?

* Am I using diet products?

* Am I relying too heavily on safe foods?

* Am I avoiding certain types of food?

* Am I incorporating risky foods?

4. **Choose a goal.** Based on your responses to the questions above, choose a reasonable goal to set for the next week. For example, "This week I will work on having breakfast."

5. **Review your progress.** At the end of each week, sit down and review your progress toward the goal you set. If it has been difficult, you may want to troubleshoot and come up with strategies to help you achieve your goal. If you reached your goal, then continue with this change and set another goal that you will work toward in the upcoming week.

6. **Remember your motivation.** This is hard work, and going through this part of recovery is challenging. It is helpful to keep in mind your reasons for wanting to overcome your eating disorder. They are what will motivate you to keep moving forward with your recovery.

7. **Reward yourself.** Give yourself credit and reward yourself for sticking to your plan and working on your goals. Rewards should not be food related. Positive rewards may include doing something fun for yourself, planning an outing with a friend, getting a new magazine (not shape or weight related!), getting a manicure, or just planning some quiet time for yourself to do something special.

8. **Focus on a positive attitude.** Don't measure your success by how you feel, as recovery is a bumpy road. Rather, measure your success by what you do. Each day that you work on your recovery or try a strategy, you are being successful. Even if a strategy backfires or you have symptoms, you can use this as an opportunity to learn about what you need to plan for next time. Keeping a positive focus will help to keep you going.

Jessica's Weekday Meal Planning Worksheet

Time	Meals and snacks	Monday	Tuesday	Wednesday	Thursday	Friday
7:30 a.m.	Breakfast	*glass o.j. 2 pieces toast with peanut butter*	*cup of tea with milk and sugar muffin orange*	*cup of tea with milk and sugar bagel with cream cheese*	*glass of grapefruit juice 2 pieces of toast with peanut butter and jam*	*tea with milk and sugar bowl of cereal banana*
	Snack (optional)					
12:30 p.m.	Lunch	*tuna sandwich with mayonnaise on a bun carrot sticks chocolate milk*	*chicken stew roll with butter cup of milk*	*chicken caesar salad vegetable soup cola*	*grilled vegetable sandwich with cheese French fries ginger ale*	*egg salad sandwich carrots and celery sticks chocolate milk*
3:30 p.m.	Snack (optional)	*banana*	*hot chocolate and a cookie*	*cheese and crackers*	*granola bar*	*coffee with cream and sugar cookie*
7:00 p.m.	Dinner	*chicken breast ½ cup rice ½ cup green beans iced tea*	*cheeseburger with side salad iced tea*	*bowl of spaghetti and meat sauce piece of garlic bread ½ cup broccoli lemonade*	*piece of fish baked potato with sour cream and chives ½ cup of peas*	*piece of roast beef, ½ cup of roast potatoes, ½ cup of corn*
9:00 p.m.	Snack (optional)	*2 cookies and glass of milk*		*piece of pie and herbal tea*	*yogurt and an apple*	*fruit salad*

Jessica's Weekend Meal Planning Worksheet

Time	Meals and snacks	Saturday	Sunday
9:00 a.m.	Breakfast	2 banana pancakes cup of tea with milk 1 sausage	2 slices of bacon 2 eggs English muffin with butter glass of o.j.
	Snack (optional)		
1:00 p.m.	Lunch	ham and cheese sandwich apple glass of milk	grilled cheese sandwich with handful of potato chips, carrot sticks, and a pickle
4:00 p.m.	Snack (optional)	Yogurt	pear
7:00 p.m.	Dinner	one portion of lasagna side salad piece of garlic bread cola piece of chocolate cake	pasta with chicken and vegetables, dinner roll side salad iced tea
10:30 p.m.	Snack (optional)		1 serving of caramel corn

Note: The sample worksheets show well-balanced non-dieting meals and snacks. If they look like too much or seem too difficult for you, remember that it may take time to get to the point where your eating looks like this. In the meantime, keep taking one step at a time.

Your Weekday Meal Planning Worksheet

Use this worksheet to plan your meals and snacks throughout the week. Record the time you will eat, what you will eat, and the amounts.

Time	Meals and snacks	Monday	Tuesday	Wednesday	Thursday	Friday
	Breakfast					
	Snack (optional)					
	Lunch					
	Snack (optional)					
	Dinner					
	Snack (optional)					

Your Weekend Meal Planning Worksheet

Use this worksheet to plan your meals and snacks for the weekend. Record the time you will eat, what you will eat, and the amounts.

Time	Meals and snacks	Saturday	Sunday
	Breakfast		
	Snack (optional)		
	Lunch		
	Snack (optional)		
	Dinner		
	Snack (optional)		

Be Prepared for the Washout Phase

When you first start to eat normally, you are likely to experience a number of physical and emotional difficulties because your system is not use to it. We use the term *washout phase* to describe this difficult time when there are no obvious benefits to the recovery process. It is typical during this phase to experience an increase in gastrointestinal discomfort and pain (bloating, gas, constipation, reflux), to feel more preoccupied with food, more dissatisfied with your body image, more anxious and depressed, and to feel strong urges to binge eat. After a while, the physical discomfort will pass, and eating normally will help to reduce your urges to binge, but at first you have to do the eating while getting no short-term benefit from it. In other words, you are likely to feel a lot worse before you feel better during the process of recovering from bulimia.

Some say that at first it is like hitting a brick wall, and many report that it is easier to engage in symptoms than to experience the intense distress associated with normalized eating. You might believe that you were better off when you were active with your eating disorder, and you may be tempted to relapse at this point. Unfortunately, there is no way around this phase. In order to get to the other side, you will need to continue with the eating, despite the discomfort. Eventually you will start to feel better.

Chapter 5

Coping Strategies

In this chapter we are going to provide you with the nuts and bolts of your recovery, the coping strategies that you need in order to avoid acting on urges for bingeing, restricting, vomiting, laxatives, overexercising and other symptoms that are related to your bulimia. To begin with, it is important to understand the difference between an urge and a symptom. An urge is an intense impulse or drive to perform a behavior that is often accompanied by negative thoughts and feelings and intense distress or discomfort. *Only when you act on the urge does it becomes a symptom.*

You might think that your urges to binge or vomit are so intense that you have to act on them or else something terrible will happen. It might help you to know that urges have a lifespan. An urge will indeed continue to increase in intensity over time, but eventually the urge will peak and start to subside and you will eventually feel better. When it comes to bulimic urges, what you need to do is to use effective coping strategies to get you through the urge. When you start this active phase of symptom interruption, it is helpful to time how long your urges last. This way, when you are faced with an intense urge, you will know how long you need to apply your coping strategies, and you will also remember that the urge will eventually pass, despite the current intensity.

What to Expect

Coping strategies are the tools that you need to use to interrupt your eating disorder symptoms and recover from bulimia; however, you should know that applying a coping strategy does not come naturally and may be very inconvenient. In the short term, it is always going to be easier and more familiar to act on urges with symptoms, because you can temporarily shut out upsetting thoughts and feelings this way. We are not denying that. But it is crucial to break the bulimic cycle by preventing symptoms, despite urges. In other words, you will no longer have the "quick fix" or immediate relief by acting on your urges, but this will pay off in the long run in terms of your recovery.

Coping strategies may make you feel a bit crazy. Consider the following example. Lynn was working on her recovery from bulimia that included overexercising as a symptom. One day, she was at home alone and had just eaten a donut as an afternoon snack. Although she had planned this food risk, her urges to exercise got very intense and she was afraid that she might act on them. She had already gotten rid of her aerobics videotapes and weights; however, she was being drawn toward the family treadmill. What she decided to do instead is to apply a coping strategy and remove herself from the situation. She stepped outside with a book and locked the door to her house. She then dropped her only house key into the mail slot of her front door. She locked herself out of her house on purpose to avoid acting on urges to exercise! She sat outside until her father returned from work and let her in. By this time, the urge to exercise had passed and she was no longer in as much danger of exercising because she was no longer alone. Now you can imagine that Lynn felt a little crazy purposely locking herself out of her own home. However, what she did was a creative and effective strategy to increase her chances of recovery from bulimia.

We will describe a number of strategies that you can apply to your bulimic urges. In reality, the possibilities are endless, and we will not be able to cover all possible strategies that might work for you. Although we will give you some guidance and hopefully some good ideas, it will be up to you to tailor the strategies so that they work for you.

Using Distraction

This coping strategy is one that you may be familiar with from your days of dieting. Many weight loss clinics and women's magazines recommend that you distract yourself when you feel like eating. Now, what we are suggesting is to flip it around and use distraction to help you avoid restriction, bingeing, vomiting, taking laxatives, and overexercise. Distraction involves engaging in an activity that will take your mind off your urges. Typically, the activity needs to be relatively enjoyable (not chores) and engaging enough to keep your mind occupied. This could include phoning a friend, taping and watching your favorite television program, doing a crossword, surfing the net, checking your e-mail, organizing photographs, doing your nails, taking a walk or a bath. This is where you have to be careful to do what works for you. For some people, watching television may trigger a binge and therefore would not be a good strategy. Similarly, some people could turn a walk into a power walk or a trip to the store for binge food. If you think a walk might be a good strategy to avoid binging, but you are afraid that you might end up in the grocery store, then take a walk but leave your wallet behind.

Sometimes you may find that you need to get out of an unsafe environment or delay going home until your urges have passed. Many people working on symptom interruption have told us about the virtues of the large bookstore. Usually these places allow you to browse and read at your leisure, and they even provide a comfortable atmosphere to do this in. One woman told us that she spent three hours in one of these bookstores one evening because she did not feel safe to go home due to strong urges to vomit.

Delaying Tactics

Delaying is a good way to learn to separate urges from behaviors. With delay, you can decide to put off acting on urges for a specified amount of time. Start with a delay of five or ten minutes. The next time you have an urge, commit to waiting ten minutes before you act on it. During that time, engage in a distracting activity. At the end of the ten minutes, reevaluate your urge and make a decision about what to do. You might decide to wait another ten minutes or to use some other strategy, or you might decide to go ahead and act on the urge. The idea behind this is that you have taken some control over whether you decide to act on the urge or not. Just because you have an urge does not mean that you have to act on that urge. After a week or so, increase the time period you commit to wait before acting on the urge. Over the next few weeks, gradually increase the delay time. Eventually you will have waited long enough to ride out the urge.

Kim used delay and distraction to avoid acting on urges to binge. She made a list of thirty different distracting activities that she could do in response to an urge to binge. She wrote each activity onto a slip of paper and folded each paper and put them into a hat. She committed to doing at least five activities that she chose randomly from the hat before acting on any urge to binge. Each activity took from five to fifteen minutes to complete. The activities that worked for Kim included painting her nails, e-mailing a friend, knitting, playing a video game, reading a chapter of her book, and playing her favorite song. If you were to use this strategy of combining delay and distraction to avoid acting on urges, what would your top ten distracting activities be? Write them in your journal for future reference, or you may even want to try Kim's hat idea.

Coping Phrases

The repetition of coping phrases may help you to avoid acting on your urges to binge, vomit, exercise, or use laxatives. A coping phrase can be a sentence or a word that is highly relevant to you and your recovery; you can say it to yourself either aloud or silently, to remind yourself of your recovery and your long-term goals. Some people write down their coping phrases onto a small piece of paper that fits into their wallet or their pocket, for easy access. Try to frame your coping statements in a positive motivating way, and stay away from statements that are punishing or harsh on yourself. Consider the following example.

Margaret was recovering from bulimia. Her main motivating factor for recovery was that she was accepted into physiotherapy school that was scheduled to begin in a few months. This was a life-long dream for Margaret and she knew that she needed to recover from her bulimia in order to function at school. The coping phrase that worked for her was "keep your eyes on the prize"; she would say this to herself whenever she felt a strong urge to binge or take laxatives. The prize of course was fulfilling her dream of becoming a physiotherapist.

Another coping phrase that works well for some people is "purging is not an option," or alternatively, "vomiting is not an option," or "laxatives are not an option." The idea behind this is that vomiting and abusing laxatives are very serious and dangerous symptoms of your bulimia. Based on this information, some people can make the commitment that purging is not an option, no matter what happens. This means that even if you binge, purging is not an option. If you can really internalize this decision not to purge, you may be surprised by the effect this has on your binge eating symptoms. If bingeing and purging usually go together for you, it may take only one binge without letting yourself purge before you learn to apply coping strategies that will prevent bingeing as well.

Below are some examples of coping phrases that people have used. But remember, it is important to tailor your personal coping phrases to something that is meaningful for you and your recovery.

* "Bingeing now will make me feel bad later on."

* "Bingeing is not an effective coping strategy in the long run."

* "Bingeing only keeps my bulimia alive."

* "This urge will pass in one hour."

* "Vomiting is not the answer to my problems."

* "Laxatives do not cause weight loss."

* "Exercise is part of my eating disorder."

* "Restricting will lead to bingeing."

* "Acting on this urge only provides temporary relief."

* "Recovery will allow me to pursue school/career/family."

* "Food is my medicine."

* "Eating food will not cause my weight to increase uncontrollably."

* "Mechanical eating will help me to stay on track."

* "I want to stick with this experiment and focus on recovery."

What are some coping phrases that might work for you?

✹ _____

✹ _____

✹ _____

High-Risk Situations

It's important to identify your high-risk situations. Many of your high-risk situations may be obvious to you, but there may be some risky situations that you are not aware of. A good way to identify these situations is to keep track of your day in terms of urges, symptoms, and what was going on right before you started to experience any urges. You can use the daily journal from chapter 2 to help track this information.

Try to pinpoint your own risky situations. Once you have clearly defined the times, places, events, and people that most often trigger symptoms, you can do one of two things: You can plan to avoid the situation if possible, or you can put strategies in place to prevent yourself from acting on urges that are triggered by these risky situations.

If possible, start off by avoiding the events and triggers that are most likely to lead to symptoms. Remember that right now while you are tying to break the bulimic cycle, it is best to make things easier for yourself. For example, if you tend to take laxatives after every time you eat at a Chinese buffet, then avoid Chinese buffets. If you end up bingeing and vomiting after you spend time with a particular weight-conscious friend, do not make plans with that person right now. Or, if you end up exercising and popping diet pills after shopping for clothes, then do not shop for clothes right now. Of course, this doesn't mean that you will never eat at a Chinese buffet, see your friend, or buy new clothes. The idea is to first normalize your eating and stop acting on urges for symptoms. Once you are feeling more confident about your recovery and your ability to avoid acting on urges, then you can add these risky situations back into your life. Through planned exposure, you can gradually confront these situations in a controlled way.

Make a Safety Plan

We know that there are some risky situations that you will not be able to avoid, no matter how hard you try. These are risky situations that are difficult, if not impossible to avoid, such as grocery shopping. For these types of situations, it is imperative that you make appropriate plans to deal with potential urges and avoid symptoms. Consider the following examples.

Every time that Gina got off the phone with her mother, she ended up exercising on her treadmill for hours. Gina decided that she needed to take control of this situation. Instead of waiting for her mom to call when Gina was not prepared, Gina started to take the initiative and call her mother at times that were convenient and safer for her. For example, she would call her mother right before she needed to be somewhere else. She also identified what was upsetting her about their phone calls, and she learned to not engage with her mother on those topics. In fact, she became quite skilled at changing the topic whenever her mother started to talk about Gina's appearance or the fact that she did not have a boyfriend.

Jason identified that whenever he experienced conflict or stress at work, he ended up bingeing on alcohol and food later that evening at home. He learned that if he had a particularly stressful day at work, it was better for him not to be at home alone. He would make plans with friends if he could, schedule a massage, go to the gym (exercise was not part of his bulimia), or go to a movie on his own. Later in the evening when he arrived home, he found that he had less time for urges to surface and that he was more relaxed due to the activity that he had participated in after work.

Grocery Shopping

Grocery shopping is a difficult and risky thing to do for most people who are struggling with and recovering from bulimia. In some ways, setting foot in a grocery store for someone recovering from bulimia is like asking a recovering alcoholic to work in a liquor store or to tend bar. The difference is that the person recovering from alcohol abuse can decide not to engage in these risky situations. You do not have this choice. You must learn to eat properly, and for most people, this includes grocery shopping.

There are several strategies that you can use to minimize the risk involved when grocery shopping:

* Make a shopping list and stick to it.

* If you have a tendency to buy binge food at the grocery store, only take enough money to buy what is on your list and leave your credit cards at home.

* If you end up bingeing on your groceries after shopping, try shopping each day for only enough food for one day of normal eating. This is very inconvenient, time consuming, and expensive, but if it prevents you from bingeing, then it is worth it.

* Grocery shop after a meal or a snack, and never go when you are hungry. Grocery shopping when you are hungry is risky because you are likely to end up with much more food in your cart than you planned, and this can set you up for bingeing.

* Try shopping with a supportive friend who is also a non-dieter and can help you relax and buy the food you need to follow your planned meal plan.

Creating a Risky Situation Hierarchy

You can use the following worksheet to get a better understanding of which situations you find the most difficult, or high risk.

Risky Situation Worksheet

Make a list of all of the specific situations that make you vulnerable for symptoms. Beside each situation, assign a risk rating from 0 to 100 using the following scale:

0————————————————50————————————————100
no risk of   moderate risk of   guaranteed to
acting on urges   acting on urges for   have symptoms
for symptoms   symptoms

Risky Situations   **Risk Rating (0–100)**

1. _____   _____

2. _____   _____

3. _____   _____

4. _____   _____

5. _____   _____

6. _____   _____

7. _____   _____

8. _____   _____

9. _____   _____

10. _____   _____

Practicing Exposure

You can start practicing exposure to the risky situations that you have identified. Reorganize your list into a hierarchy so the items with the lowest ratings are at the bottom. This is a good place to start because the risk of symptoms associated with the situation is more manageable than situations higher up on your list. Use the following worksheet to help you practice confronting the situation in a controlled and planned way. Make plenty of copies before you begin.

As you continue to expose yourself to the risky situation, you should notice that your risk level for symptoms decreases. Once your risk level is reduced to a rating of 20 or less, move on to the next situation on your hierarchy. In this manner, you will gradually work your way up your hierarchy over time. Through this exposure process, you will learn what strategies work for you and will gain confidence in your ability to manage stressful situations, without resorting to symptoms.

Risky Situation Planning Worksheet

Record the situation and urges that you are preparing to confront. Write down a safety plan and a back-up safety plan and the date you will do the exposure. After the exposure, go back to the worksheet, and write about the outcome.

What is the situation? _____

_____

_____

What are your expected urges? _____

_____

Specific safety plan: How will you manage this situation? What strategies will you use?

_____

_____

_____

_____

Back-up safety plan: If your initial safety plan does not work out, what alternate strategies will you use?

_____

_____

_____

_____

Date of exposure practice: _____

Outcome: How well did your plan work? What did you learn from this exposure practice?

_____

_____

_____

_____

Revised plan for next time: Based on your exposure practice, what do you need to change in your safety plan for the next time you practice this situation?

_____

_____

_____

_____

Breaking the Habit

Some people have described that when they are having symptoms, it is like being in a fog or a daze. Jill described not really being fully aware and present during her binge eating and vomiting episodes: "One minute I would be sitting on the couch worrying about an upcoming exam, and it felt like the next minute I had my head in the toilet vomiting a binge." Other people describe symptoms as being very habitual. Some say that they don't feel urges anymore, rather they binge because it is Saturday, or they take laxatives because it has been three days since their last dose, or they vomit because they ate pizza. In these examples, people are behaving like they are on automatic pilot.

Whatever the case, typically each symptom is a series of smaller steps involving decisions that are conscious and deliberate. For example, when Jill acts on urges and has a binge and vomit episode, her symptoms can be broken down into much smaller steps:

1. Get off couch.

2. Check to see if anyone is home.

3. Walk to kitchen.

4. Open cupboard.

5. Get out peanut butter.

6. Open jar.

7. Open bread box.

8. Get out bread.

9. Open drawer.

10. Get knife.

11. Spread peanut butter.

12. Eat each piece of bread and peanut butter.

13. Go to bathroom.

14. Bend over toilet.

15. Use finger to vomit once.

16. Vomit again.

Although most binge and vomit episodes probably include more steps than this, you get the idea.

Remember, a symptom can be interrupted at any time. At any step, you can decide not to continue with the symptom sequence and to try an alternative route or distraction. For example, Jill might decide to close the cupboard door and go phone a friend rather than get the peanut butter out at step four. Or she could decide to stop eating halfway through the loaf of bread and go outside for a leisurely walk at step 12. Or, she could decide to leave the bathroom at step 14 or step 15.

If you do binge, you can still break the binge-purge cycle and decide not to vomit, take laxatives, or exercise. An urge does not have to lead to a symptom, and starting a symptom does not have to lead to the completion of that symptom. You can decide at any point during the chain of events that make up a symptom to stop and do something different. Raising your awareness, and not acting on urges or continuing with symptoms automatically, is an important part of your recovery.

Raising Your Awareness Worksheet

Think about the last symptom you had and break it down into smaller steps. At each step, specify an alternative activity that you could choose to do, instead of continuing with the next step in the symptom sequence.

Symptom: _____

Symptom Sequence   **Alternative Activity**

Step 1 _____   OR _____

Step 2 _____   OR _____

Step 3 _____   OR _____

Step 4 _____   OR _____

Step 5 _____   OR _____

Step 6 _____   OR _____

Step 7 _____   OR _____

Step 8 _____   OR _____

Step 9 _____   OR _____

Step 10 _____   OR _____

Step 11 _____   OR _____

Step 12 _____   OR _____

Step 13 _____   OR _____

Step 14 _____   OR _____

Step 15 _____   OR _____

Step 16 _____   OR _____

Step 17 _____   OR _____

Step 18 _____   OR _____

Making Your Environment Safe

In order to maximize your chances of recovery, it is important to make your environment safe and free from any dieting and eating disorder-related paraphernalia, such as:

* diet products

* binge foods

* laxatives

* diet pills

* fashion and exercise magazines

* workout equipment and videos

* your gym membership (ask to put it on hold for health reasons)

* measuring tapes

* bathroom scales

* calorie counting books

* measuring cups

* anything that you use to help you vomit

* "thin" or "fat" pictures that you use as inspiration not to eat

* clothing that is too small.

Ideally, it would be great if you could take inventory of your place, identify every item that plays a role in your eating disorder, and discard it immediately. We know that it is not that easy, however.

Take small clothing. It is not uncommon for someone with bulimia to have a variety of different sizes of clothing in the wardrobe. This reflects the frequent weight fluctuations that are a result of dieting and bingeing. You may be holding on to your smaller sizes because you have a strong desire to fit back into them, or you may be using a particular piece of clothing to gauge your body size. Either way, this is a serious problem and is likely to cause strong urges to diet and to lose weight.

Although it would be best to gather up all such pieces of clothing and toss them away, we know that this is a very difficult thing to do. If you are not ready to throw your small clothing away, then we suggest that you place them out of sight. If you can muster the strength to give your clothing away, we recommend that you give it to someone who you will never see wearing it. Just imagine what it would be like to see your sister or your best friend wearing your favorite pair of jeans that no longer fit you! If you are worried about the money you spent on a wardrobe that no longer fits, you might try to sell your clothing at a consignment store. Keeping the clothes to torture yourself is a bad investment!

We know that the act of gathering up and getting rid of your small clothing can lead to negative thoughts about your body and might produce urges to binge, vomit, exercise, diet, or take laxatives. Try to avoid trying on clothing that you know no longer fits, and ask a supportive friend or family member to help you with this chore.

When you are recovering from bulimia, you need comfortable clothing that fits you. Invest in some new outfits. Remember that shopping for clothing can be a risk in and of itself so be sure to plan appropriately for any shopping trips.

You also might want to give up your bathroom scale to increase the safety of your environment. Scales are treacherous. In one study, a scale was manipulated so that some chronic dieters believed they had gained five pounds (when they really had not). When the dieters believed that they had gained weight, they felt more depressed and anxious, felt worse about themselves, and they actually ate more than when they believed that their weight had not changed (McFarlane, Polivy, and Herman 1998).

To make your environment safer, you can also adjust what you do in your daily routine. If you are likely to vomit after meals, then make sure you use the bathroom before you eat and stay away from it after eating. If you buy laxatives on your way home from school or work, then find a new route home that does not include a pharmacy. And, if your walk to the grocery store frequently turns into a power walk and a calorie-burning mission, then take public transportation or arrange to get a ride. Take time now to take stock of your environment and daily routines and think about what you can do to make your environment as safe and as low risk as possible. Complete the following worksheet, and try to maximize your chances for recovery.

Environmental Inventory Worksheet

After taking a close look at your environment, what are the eating disorder and dieting- related items that might make your environment unsafe or make you vulnerable for symptoms?

_____

_____

_____

_____

_____

_____

What daily routines may interfere with your recovery?

_____

_____

_____

What can you do over the next week to help focus your environment and your routine on recovery? Refer back to your inventory each week and decide what additional steps you can take.

_____

_____

_____

_____

Limiting the Opportunities

You can limit the times and opportunities that you allow yourself to have symptoms. Eventually, having symptoms becomes much too inconvenient or unpleasant and it becomes easier to avoid symptoms than to have them. This is exactly how many smokers end up quitting. As the rules and norms around smoking become increasingly strict, many smokers are limited to smoking outside, regardless of the weather. For some people, this inconvenience and unpleasantness is enough to stop smoking. Obviously, this strategy takes an enormous amount of commitment when you have to impose such sanctions on yourself. Examples include allowing yourself to binge only in the garage or on one type of food, allowing yourself to vomit only in one toilet in the basement, allowing yourself to buy laxatives only at one store that is located an hour away, or allowing yourself to attend only one exercise class daily that begins at 5:00 A.M.

Acting with Mindfulness

Mindfulness is perhaps more of a philosophy than a strategy. Mindfulness is a type of meditation that involves staying in the moment. "Mindfulness means paying attention in a particular way: on purpose, in the present moment, and nonjudgementally" (Kabat-Zinn 1994, p.4.). This includes letting go of anxious thoughts about the past or the future. Thoughts are quietly observed, not judged or engaged. Mindfulness is currently used for stress reduction, pain management, coping with chronic illnesses (Kabat-Zinn 1990) and preventing relapse in depression (Segal, Williams, and Teasdale 2002). Some describe it as a way to take control of your mind, rather than allowing your mind to control you, and for this reason, it may be helpful in controlling your symptoms.

Try the following exercise to practice being mindful. This exercise is based on the work of Jon Kabat-Zinn (1990). Be prepared that it looks easier than it is, and that at times, mindfulness practice can be stressful.

1. Make sure you are wearing comfortable clothing.

2. Find a comfortable spot, where you will not be interrupted for five minutes.

3. Sit or lie down.

4. Close your eyes if this feels comfortable.

5. Bring your attention to your breathing. Focus your attention on how it feels to breathe. Focus on how your body changes as you inhale and as you exhale. Feel the air passing through your nostrils and your mouth as you inhale and exhale. Feel your diaphragm rise or expand as you inhale and fall as you exhale.

6. Pay attention to what is happening in this moment as you continue to breathe. Stay with your breathing. Inhaling and exhaling. Inhaling and exhaling.

7. Every time that you notice that your mind has wandered, and it will, acknowledge the thought, let it go, and bring your attention back to your breathing.

8. Observe your thoughts; do not judge them or engage them.

9. Every time your mind wanders, acknowledge the thought, let it go, and bring your attention back to your breathing.

Do this exercise for five or ten minutes. Afterwards, record your experience in your journal. Include your thoughts and feelings and any obstacles you encountered.

Complete this exercise daily for one week.

This mindfulness exercise will help you to practice *being* rather than *doing*, and can have a profound impact on how you see yourself, other people, and the world around you. If you practice these skills regularly, you can use them in your daily life. When your mind is racing, when you notice your anxiety level rise, or when urges for symptoms become strong, you can remind yourself to be mindful. Pay attention to your breathing and connect with the moment. Acknowledge and observe thoughts without judging them or engaging in them. Just because you think it, does not make it true.

It is also possible to practice this skill by performing daily activities mindfully. For example, you may decide to drive, clean the house, or interact with your family mindfully. Pay attention to what is going on in the moment, and observe and let go of any other thoughts. Mindfulness skills can calm your mind, reduce stress, and may even help with symptom management. For those of you who are interested in this philosophy, and would like to explore it further, we encourage you to read the book *Full Catastrophe Living* by Jon Kabat-Zinn (1990). In this book, Kabat-Zinn recommends daily meditation practice of 45 minutes, and includes other exercises such as yoga and walking meditation.

Having a Good Defense

Separating your urges from actual symptoms and applying coping strategies are a critical part of your recovery. If it feels like hard work, then you are probably doing it right, for coping strategies are not natural or easy to use.

Remember, when it comes to fighting urges to binge, the first line of defense is to follow a well-balanced meal plan and to avoid feeling physically or psychologically deprived of food. Use the strategies described in chapter 4 to avoid restricting your food intake (such as, mechanical eating, treating food as medicine). Don't be surprised if urges to binge continue. Most people have a variety of risky situations that can trigger urges to binge, only one of which is hunger or deprivation. This is why you need to have coping strategies to avoid acting on urges to binge and other symptoms. Experiment with different strategies until you find those that will work for you. Ideally, you can develop a battery of strategies that you can draw upon during difficult times throughout your recovery.

Chapter 6

Shifting Eating
Disordered Thoughts

So far, we have been teaching you strategies for controlling what you do in response to eating disorder urges. Now it's time to focus on how you think about yourself. By paying attention to your eating disorder thoughts and learning how to shift your thinking patterns, you can learn a powerful method to change how you feel.

Thinking Distortions

Reality is subjective. If five people witness a car accident, they will have five different views of what happened. The bystanders' views of reality are distorted by the details that they paid attention to, how they processed the event in their minds, and how their view was influenced by their own experiences, values, and beliefs.

Typically, some amount of cognitive distortion is normal. However, when your view of the world becomes extremely distorted or when your distortions are rigid and inflexible, you become vulnerable to experiencing emotional disturbance (Beck 1976). Although you cannot necessarily change what life throws your way, you can choose how you will react to a situation and what view you will take of it (Ellis 1962). The idea that emotional disturbance is caused by distorted or dysfunctional thinking patterns and that you can change how you feel by changing how you think forms the guiding principle of cognitive therapy. Cognitive therapy is an approach developed initially for depression by Aaron T. Beck in the early 1960s (Beck 1964) and later expanded to a wide range of psychological problems and populations, including eating disorders (Fairburn, Marcus, and Wilson 1993). The strategies in this chapter are based on the work of a number of pioneers in this field, including Aaron Beck (1976), Judith Beck (1995), David Burns (1999), and Dennis Greenberger and Christine Padesky (1995).

Eating Disorder Thoughts

We use the term *eating disorder thoughts* to describe the type of cognitive distortions related to your eating disorder. Eating disorder thoughts include attitudes, beliefs, interpretations, predictions, images, or rules that are in some way dominated by themes related to weight, shape, appearance, and unhealthy eating patterns. By contrast, non-eating disorder thoughts are thoughts that are not heavily burdened by themes of weight, shape, appearance, and eating patterns. Non-eating disorder thoughts are characterized by a more balanced and realistic view.

Consider the following case. Jane is a twenty-six-year-old woman who was reviewing her week with her therapist. When they were going over her eating for the week, Jane reported, "I had one piece of cake and felt like I had gained fifty pounds! I felt so horrible and out of control that I had to go throw it up." Later in the session, Jane reported, "I am only going to eat one meal a day. That way I will feel in control and feel good about myself." This rule of only eating once per day was triggered by an incident that had happened the day before. Jane was out at a bar with her boyfriend and they were listening to some music. Jane couldn't help noticing that there were lots of attractive women in the bar. Jane began to worry that her boyfriend might find someone more interesting and attractive then her. She began to feel bad about herself: "I felt so fat and disgusting. It makes me worried that he is going to find someone else thinner then me. I have to do something about that. I need to lose some weight."

You can look at Jane's eating disorder thoughts and examine them for distortions by comparing them to a more realistic view of the situation.

Jane's Eating Disorder Thoughts	Realistic View
I had one piece of cake and felt like I had gained fifty pounds!	You can't gain fifty pounds from a piece of cake. Just because it feels this way doesn't mean that it is true.
I felt so horrible and out of control that I had to go throw it up.	Having rigid eating rules sets you up to feel out of control when you break them. Just because you broke an eating rule, doesn't mean you are an out-of-control person. Just because you eat a piece of cake, doesn't mean you *have* to go and throw it up.
I am only going to eat one meal a day. That way I will feel in control and feel good about myself.	Eating only one meal a day is not a normal, healthy plan. It is an unhealthy strategy aimed at trying to feel in control. There are probably healthier strategies you can use to feel better about yourself. Eating one meal a day will set you up for urges to binge later.
I felt so fat and disgusting.	Just because you feel fat doesn't mean you are fat. Just because you feel disgusting, doesn't mean you are disgusting. Feeling fat and disgusting when your boyfriend sees attractive women is a sign that you are feeling insecure in the relationship, not that there is something really wrong with you.
It makes me worried that he is going to find someone else thinner then me.	Just because you are focused on thinness and appearance doesn't necessarily mean that your boyfriend is too. He is probably listening to the music at the bar and it is unlikely that he is comparing you to every girl in the place.
I have to do something about that. I need to lose some weight.	If the real problem is feeling insecure about your relationship, losing weight to fix the relationship doesn't seem like an appropriate solution. What does your weight have to do with the relationship?

Common Thought Distortions

The following thought distortions are ones we commonly see among people with bulimia. We have listed several categories of distortions. You may find that your thoughts will fit into more than one category.

Emotional Reasoning

Emotional reasoning involves believing something is true because you feel it is true (Burns 1999). For example, Jennifer woke up one day and was feeling very down. She thought, "I am a useless person." This thought led her to feel even worse about herself and also motivated her to feel better using unhealthy coping strategies. She decided she would only eat one small meal that day and she canceled her plans to go out. When we examined this experience in therapy, we focused on her thought, "I am a useless person."

We challenged Jennifer to come up with some evidence that she was really useless. She had difficulty coming up with any evidence. Then we challenged Jennifer to come up with evidence that she was not useless. She came up with a number of important facts, including the following: "I do a good job at work." "The kids I teach like me." "My boyfriend tells me I am wonderful." "My parents are always telling me I do too much, which is the opposite of being useless."

Like Jennifer, as you start to identify your thoughts and consider the evidence based on your own experience of whether the thought is true, you will find that over time and with practice, the distorted thought will become less believable.

Thinking by the Scale

With bulimia, the number on the scale can determine your sense of self-worth. You would probably think it was ludicrous if I measured how I felt based on how tall I was or my shoe size. You would probably never measure any person's worth by what they weigh, but yet you may do this to yourself all the time.

The belief that you can change how you feel inside by changing your body size or weight is a very powerful distortion. It is also a magical distortion commonly used by the weight loss companies to sell a dream. Think of a popular weight loss product or method. You have probably seen the before and after pictures that they use. The before picture shows someone who looks like she just made it through a hard day at work or perhaps just woke up. She is sloppily dressed, wearily posed, and looks like she needs to do some self-care with her personal hygiene. The after picture shows someone who looks like she just came out of the salon. She is professionally made up, smartly dressed, and appears bright-eyed and excited. She is usually shown beside a fancy car or an attractive member of the opposite sex. The message is that if you lose weight, you will receive a complete makeover, a fancy car, a wonderful partner, and success. Most importantly, you will be happy. The reality is that you can have all these things without losing weight because they are not connected!

You have probably had the thought, "If I just lose five pounds, things would be different." This is a common eating disorder thought. What people find is that when they get there, five pounds lighter, nothing around them or inside them has really changed, but instead of realizing that losing weight isn't the answer to their problems, they think, "I just need to lose a bit more." And so the magical thinking continues.

Social Comparison

Individuals with eating disorders commonly engage in social comparison, where they compare themselves to other people on different aspects, usually body weight, size, shape, and appearance. This strategy becomes problematic when you always lose out on the comparison. When every comparison you make results in seeing someone else as thinner, better looking, more disciplined, and more successful, you are guaranteed to feel worse about yourself. It is also a cognitive distortion. You select targets for comparison that set you up to feel bad, or you selectively focus on the positive aspects of other people and the negative aspects of yourself.

Social comparison occurs when you are unsure about yourself in some aspect, so you compare yourself to others to see how you are doing. One strategy to counteract social comparison is to think of yourself as an island. You are your own person and worthwhile just the way you are. You don't need to compare yourself to other people. It really doesn't matter how they look, how much they weigh, or what they are doing.

Feeling Fat

"I feel fat" is a very common eating disorder thought. Why do we have it here as a thought distortion? Well, what does "I feel fat" really mean? *Fat* is not a feeling. Rather, the phrase "I feel fat" is really a mask for a host of very real and painful feelings such as being sad, hopeless, disgusted, dejected, incompetent, frustrated, and worthless. It is easier to say "I feel fat" to describe these painful emotions than to really examine how you might feel. Also, if you are feeling fat, you know what to do to feel better—restrict your eating and diet—whereas if you are feeling sad, hopeless, disgusted, and incompetent, it is probably overwhelming because it is not clear how to feel better. So feeling fat reflects an emotional state; it is not an objective reflection of your weight.

Consider the following examples:

Jan wakes up and is feeling really good. She is looking forward to the day. Before she gets dressed, she steps on the scale. Suddenly, she feels completely different. She feels fat and her day is ruined.

Barb has a great day at work and is looking forward to seeing a movie with a friend that evening. When she gets home, there is a message from the friend saying that he has to cancel. Barb is angry for a second, but then realizes that she is too fat to have reliable friends. Her friend probably found someone more attractive and fun to go out with.

Kate is out shopping with a very thin girlfriend. As they are going through the stores, her girlfriend tries on everything in sight. Kate has trouble finding clothes that fit nicely. Over the course of the day, she feels increasingly fat.

These stories illustrate people who are generally going through their day feeling good until something triggers them to feel bad about themselves. This feeling is translated almost instantaneously into feeling fat. Of course, their actual body size hasn't really changed in an instant, and herein is where the distortion lies. What has changed in an instant is how they feel about themselves.

Thinking in Extremes

Thinking in extremes, or all-or-nothing thinking, is a common thought distortion (Burns 1999). For people with eating disorders, it usually takes the following forms: There are only good foods or bad foods; you are a good person or a bad - person; you are fat or thin; you stick to your diet or you are completely off. The strategy for counteracting extreme thinking is to consider a more balanced perspective.

For example, Larissa had been symptom-free for three weeks. She had not binged or purged and had kept her eating on track. She was feeling very good about her recovery. One evening she was getting ready to go out and the outfit she was planning to wear was too tight. She thought to herself, "I am too fat and I need to start restricting my eating." The next day, she didn't eat for the whole day. By the evening, she was fighting strong urges to binge. Eventually she gave in to the urges and binged, finishing by vomiting in the bathroom to get rid of what she had eaten. Larissa's extreme interpretation of her outfit not fitting right set her up for symptoms.

Can you come up with some more realistic or balanced interpretations of the situation? How would a person without an eating disorder have reacted?

Here are some possibilities:

* "I am not too fat. My weight is just fluctuating because I am in recovery and that is a positive step."

* "Looks like I need to get a new outfit."

* "Although I have urges to restrict my eating, that is just the eating disorder taking over. I will sit with the urges and they will pass."

Harsh Self Judgment

People with eating disorders commonly judge themselves harshly. Your inner voice is often negative, running you down: "You are fat and disgusting"; "you have no self-control"; "you are ugly and a loser"; "you need to get it together"; "you are stupid"; "you can't do anything right"; "you are unlovable." Of course, you would never say any of these things to someone you loved. Yet for some reason, it is okay to say them to yourself. Harsh self-judgment is a distortion because it is always negative, and the statements are not realistic. Harsh self-judgment results in further erosion of your self-worth and fuels efforts to feel better by changing your weight and shape.

Identifying Your Problematic Thoughts

You are always thinking, even when you are not aware of it. Thoughts are triggered by situations, by other thoughts, by feelings, and by behaviors. For every trigger, you have a corresponding thought process or interpretation. The first step in shifting your thought patterns is to become more aware of your thoughts, and in particular, your problematic thoughts, associated with a negative emotion such as feelings of shame, guilt, sadness, anger, depression, and incompetence. Problematic thoughts occur when you have urges for eating disorder symptoms. When you are feeling a negative emotion or having urges for eating disorder symptoms, it is a good time to look inward and examine what thoughts are going through your mind. Use the following worksheet to monitor your eating disorder thoughts. First look at the example.

Thought Monitoring Example

Feeling(s) and Urges Rate (0–100)	Situation/Trigger	Thoughts	Distortions
guilty (80) *out of control (70)*	*Went to a birthday party and had a large piece of chocolate cake.*	*I shouldn't have eaten that.* *I am a pig.*	*thinking in extremes* *harsh self-judgment/ emotional reasoning*
worthless (90) *depressed (90)* *urge to binge (90)*	*Fight with boyfriend because he said he couldn't drive down to see me for the weekend.*	*He isn't coming because he doesn't love me anymore.* *I feel fat and unattractive.* *He will find someone else.* *I might as well binge.*	*thinking in extremes* *feeling fat* *emotional reasoning* *thinking in extremes*
Fat = *disgusting (60); incompetent (80); overwhelmed (90); frustrated (60); depressed (40); uncomfortable (90)* *urge to restrict my eating (95)*	*At party with boyfriend and run into his ex. She is very thin and beautiful. She is in medical school. They have a long conversation.*	*She is much thinner and more successful than me.* *I feel fat and ugly.* *I am a loser.* *I want to get out of here.* *I wish we hadn't run into her.* *I don't measure up.* *I need to lose weight.*	*social comparison* *feeling fat/emotional reasoning* *harsh self-judgment* *thinking in extremes* *emotional reasoning/ social comparison* *thinking by the scale*

Thought Monitoring Worksheet

Over the next week, use this worksheet to monitor your thoughts whenever you notice a downward shift in how you are feeling or when you have urges for eating disorder symptoms. Record what feelings you are experiencing and the intensity of each feeling from 0 (not at all) to 100 (most extreme). Record the situation or trigger associated with the feeling(s). Record any thoughts that were going through your mind at the time. Examine the thoughts you had for any distortions and record them. Identify as many distortions as you can for each thought.

Feeling(s) and Urges Rate (0–100)	Situation/Trigger	Thoughts	Distortions

Thought Monitoring Review

After you have monitored your thoughts for a week, look for connections between your feelings and thoughts, and the situations or triggers. Are there common triggers or situations?

_____

_____

_____

_____

Do you see any recurring thought distortions?

_____

_____

_____

_____

If you have difficulty identifying your thoughts or thought distortions, continue monitoring for another week. As you become more aware of the connection between situations and your thoughts and feelings, it will become easier to identify problematic thoughts and thought distortions.

Shifting Your Problematic Thoughts

Now that you are aware of the connection between your thoughts and feelings and situations or triggers and you are able to identify your problematic thoughts and thought distortions, you are ready for the next step: shifting your problematic thoughts. The goal here is to widen your perspective so that you can come up with a more balanced or realistic view. This technique of shifting your thinking doesn't lead to results overnight, but over time you will find that you are no longer reacting to triggers in the same way. You will also notice that you have more control over how you *choose* to react to a situation. Practice counteracting your eating disorder thoughts using the Shifting Problematic Thoughts worksheet. Make copies so you can complete the worksheet whenever you notice a fluctuation in your mood or urges for eating disorder symptoms. We've also provided you with a couple of examples.

Note: If you have trouble generating alternative ways of thinking about the situation (the "realistic view"), then ask yourself the following questions:

* How would someone without an eating disorder think about this situation?

✸ What are alternative ways of interpreting this situation?

✸ What would I say to a friend who felt this way?

✸ How do these thoughts fit with my values and goals in life and what is important to me as a person?

✸ How useful is this way of thinking?

✸ What impact does this way of thinking have on my life?

Shifting Problematic Thoughts Example

Feeling(s) and Urges Rate (0–100)	Situation or Trigger	Problematic Thoughts	Realistic View	Rerate Feelings (0–100)	Outcome
guilty (80) out of control (70)	Went to a birthday party and had a large piece of chocolate cake.	I shouldn't have eaten that. I am a pig.	It is normal to have a piece of birthday cake at a party. This fits into my eating plan as a normal dessert. Maybe the portion was a bit larger than normal, but that is okay. I wouldn't call a friend a pig so it is not okay to call myself one. Just because I feel that way doesn't mean it is true. This is really about a deeper issue (not a piece of cake), which is I don't feel very good about myself.	guilty (20) out of control (30)	Was able to socialize and actually enjoy myself instead of leaving early like I would have in the past!

worthless (90) depressed (90) disap-pointed (90) urge to binge (95)	Fight with boyfriend because he said he couldn't drive down to see me for the weekend.	He isn't coming because he doesn't love me anymore. I feel fat and unattractive. He will find someone else. I might as well binge.	There are more reasonable explanations of why he isn't coming (he has a big exam to study for). Just because he isn't coming doesn't mean he doesn't love me. There are lots of examples of how he really does love me. I am just feeling a bit insecure in the relationship and this is making me feel bad about myself. Obviously he finds me attractive, or he wouldn't be going out with me. Long-distance relationships are stressful. It is okay to be disappointed that I won't see him. Bingeing is only a temporary solution. I will feel worse afterwards for having symptoms when I am trying to work on recovery.	worthless (20) depres-sed (50) disap-pointed (90) urge to binge (60)	Make alterna-tive plan for the weekend. I will call some girl-friends and do some-thing fun.
fat = disgusting (60) incompe-tent (80) over-whelmed (90) frustrated (60) depressed (40) uncom-fortable (90) urge to restrict my eating (95)	At party with boyfriend and run into his ex. She is very thin and beautiful. She is in medical school. They have a long conversa-tion.	She is much thinner and more successful than me. I feel fat and ugly. I am a loser. I want to get out of here. I wish we didn't run into her. I don't measure up. I need to lose weight.	It doesn't matter what she looks like or what she does. I am my own person. I have my own strengths. Fat is not a feeling. I am feeling bad about myself and insecure in my relationship. This is not about how I look. Just because I feel ugly doesn't mean I am. I am not a loser even if I feel like one at this moment. I wouldn't call my friend a loser, so I won't call myself one either. I am just being harsh with myself. What am I measuring anyway? I am not even sure of the standard I am comparing myself to, which is unrealistic. I still wish we didn't run into her. It is normal to feel uncomfortable in this type of situation. It is okay to feel uncomfortable. Losing weight won't really change the way I feel inside.	fat = disgusting (20) incom-petent (30) over-whelmed (40) frustrated (40) depres-sed (10) uncom-fortable (75) urge to restrict my eating (50)	Excused myself from the conver-sation and went and talked to some other people I knew. Shifted the focus off of her and on to other people.

Shifting Problematic Thoughts Worksheet

Over the next week, use this sheet to monitor your thoughts and counteract problematic or eating disorder thoughts whenever you notice a downward shift in how you are feeling or urges to have symptoms. Record what feelings you are experiencing and the intensity of each feeling from 0 (not at all) to 100 (most extreme). Record the situation or trigger associated with the feeling(s). Record any thoughts that were going through your mind at the time. Examine the thoughts for any distortions. Counteract the distortions or eating disorder thoughts. Rerate your feelings (0 to 100) and then record the outcome or how you responded to the situation or trigger.

Feeling(s) and Urges Rate (0–100)	Situation or Trigger	Problematic Thoughts	Realistic View (How would someone without an eating disorder think about this situation? What are alternative ways of interpreting this situation? What would I say to a friend who felt this way? How do these thoughts fit with my values and goals in life and what is important to me as a person? How useful is this way of thinking? What impact does this way of thinking have on me?)	Rerate Feelings (0–100)	Outcome

Shifting Problematic Thoughts Review

After you have practiced counteracting your problematic thoughts for a week, are there any counteracting thoughts that are particularly useful or powerful for you (for example, "I am an island," "Just because I feel it, doesn't mean it is true," "Fat is not a feeling," "It is okay to have these feelings," "I am a worthwhile person")?

_____

_____

_____

Did you notice your mood shift depending on what you were thinking?

_____

_____

_____

Troubleshooting

When you first start counteracting problematic thoughts, you may find that you don't experience drastic shifts in your emotions right away. That is because you don't yet believe your alternative views. As you continue practicing, you will find that it gets easier. You will also become more aware of the distortions in your eating disorder thoughts. As these changes occur, you will gradually start to feel better and feel more in control.

With continued practice, you will also find that you are able to shift your thoughts without using the worksheet. At that point, you may prefer to do this exercise in your head. On the other hand, if you feel better when you write it out, go ahead and do so. Choose the method that works the best for you.

Chapter 7

Feeling Better about Your Body

In the early stages of recovery, it is normal to feel worse about your body as you normalize your eating and deal with the fear that your weight will go out of control. Body image work is really the long-term work of recovery from an eating disorder. Our goals at this point are to help you

1. consider the deeper role that body image plays in your life;

2. learn to tolerate negative body image without acting on your feelings with eating disorder symptoms;

3. begin to establish a new and healthy relationship with your body where you are able to appreciate your body for reasons other than just appearance.

When you think about it, most people in our society feel dissatisfied in some way with their bodies. One study found that 79 percent of young girls aged eleven to twelve reported wanting to be thinner (Maloney et al. 1989). There is also research showing that a significant proportion of young boys also want to be thinner (Ricciardelli and McCabe 2001). Thus, the statistics tell us it is *normal* or common to feel badly about your body.

Understanding Your Body Image

The media plays a major role in fueling body dissatisfaction; the images projected in all forms of media portray an unattainable and unrealistic beauty ideal. For women, the ideal is a very thin body, a shape that corresponds to reality for only 2 or 3 percent of women (Statistics Canada 2001). For men, the ideal is a very muscularly built and sculpted body with minimal body fat. These media images create an environment where people are unable to measure up, resulting in body dissatisfaction.

Many people take some degree of body dissatisfaction in stride, so it doesn't have a major impact on their lives. For people with an eating disorder, it is a different story. Feeling badly about your body plays a central role in your life and crowds out other interests and activities. Why is body image much more important to some people than it is to others? One big factor in determining the importance of your body image, as you have probably guessed, is your self-esteem. If you feel good or worthwhile about yourself overall, you will be less concerned with negative feelings that you may have about your body because your body does not define who you are as a person.

When you feel badly about yourself, or when you think you have little to offer, you may focus those feelings on your body. Your body is a good target for several reasons. Sometimes it is too painful to acknowledge your true feelings and insecurities; blaming your body for your problems is less threatening. Also, focusing on your body may distract you from larger problems that do not have identifiable solutions. Feeling badly about your body is more acceptable because there appears to be a clear solution to negative body image: changing your body. One thing we do know is that feeling badly about your body or wanting to lose weight is usually never *just* about your body. Rather, other issues are almost always involved (Jasper 1993).

Savita's Story

Savita grew up in an unstable home environment. Her mother died of cancer when she was a baby, leaving her dad to raise her and her brother on his own. Her dad remarried when she was five, but the marriage ended in divorce when she was thirteen. Around this time, Savita began to hate her body, feeling that she was too fat. Strict dieting led to bingeing, vomiting, and overexercising, and so began her struggle with bulimia.

For Savita, a number of factors led to her poor body image. Her home environment was stressful and she felt partly responsible for her father's divorce. Growing up, she had always felt insecure and worried constantly about losing her dad, as she had lost her mother. She had viewed her stepmother as her mom, and the divorce meant a big loss for her, contributing to her feelings of insecurity. She described feeling helpless. Focusing on her body and losing weight made her feel like she was more effective and in control of something in her life. Also, acknowledging her feelings of sadness connected to the divorce was very threatening and painful for Savita, and it was much safer to translate the sadness into "feeling fat." It wasn't clear for Savita how to handle another loss, but she knew what to do in response to feeling fat. Savita's eating disorder was about much more than just being thin; it gave her false feelings of security, and increased feelings of control in her life, and protection from emotional pain.

Your Story

It is important to identify your thoughts and feelings about your body and to get a better understanding of the role negative body image plays in your life.

What are your thoughts about your body? What do you dislike? What do you like?

_____

_____

_____

_____

What are your feelings about your body?

_____

_____

_____

_____

What are some of the reasons *why* your body image may be so important to you? What role does your body image play in your life?

_____

_____

_____

_____

What factors (key events, experiences, and social interactions) have contributed to your negative body image?

_____

_____

_____

_____

Think back to when your body image started to really bother you or interfere with your life. What other things were going on in your life at that time? What stressors, emotions, and thoughts about yourself were you dealing with?

_____

_____

_____

_____

What Do Thin and Fat Mean to You?

To further understand the role body image plays in your life, you need to examine what "being thin" or "being fat" really means to you. It may go beyond body size. In fact, research shows that children as young as seven associate *fat* with bad and *thin* with good. Studies have found that young girls and boys rated obese children as being less popular, less happy, less successful at school, and being lazier than average and thinner children (Tiggemann and Wilson-Barrett 1998).

For Savita being thin meant feeling in control, successful, attractive, happy, and worthwhile, whereas being fat meant she was weak, insufficient, ugly, unhappy, and out of control. Here are some other examples of what "being fat" might really mean:

sad	disgusted
incompetent	worthless
frustrated	angry
exasperated	hopeless
depressed	dejected
anxious	scared
frightened	overwhelmed
guilty	humiliated
ashamed	lonely

What does being "thin" means to you?

_____

_____

_____

_____

What does being "fat" means to you?

_____

_____

_____

_____

Now examine the connections that you have made. Are they really true?

_____

_____

_____

_____

Are the qualities that you have written in the blanks really dependent on your body size or shape?

_____

_____

_____

_____

How Do You Feel about Your Body?

Before we get started with active strategies, it is helpful to take a rating of how negative or positive you feel about your body right now. As you go through the exercises in this chapter, your ratings may start to shift. At the end of the chapter, you can rate your feelings about your body again to assess your progress.

Negative Body Feelings

Over the past week, how negative have you felt about your body? Rate your general level of negative feelings from 0 to 100, where 0 means you feel neutral (no negative feelings about your body at all) and 100 means you absolutely despise your body.

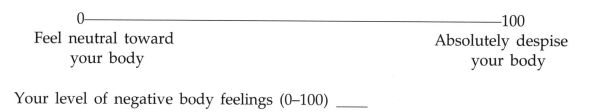

Your level of negative body feelings (0–100) ____

Positive Body Feelings

Over the past week, how positive have you felt about your body? Rate your general level of positive feelings from 0 to 100, where 0 means you feel neutral (no positive feelings about your body at all) and 100 means you feel very positive and comfortable with your body.

0————————————————————————————100
Feel neutral toward   Absolutely despise
    your body   your body

Your level of positive body feelings (0–100) ____

Developing a Healthy Relationship with Your Body

Now that you have a better understanding of your negative body image, you are ready to start to develop a healthier relationship with your body. First of all, we want to review some coping strategies that will help you manage your negative feelings about your body and develop more neutral feelings.

Get Rid of Clothes That Don't Fit

Getting rid of unrealistically thin clothing or clothes that you use to measure yourself (a certain belt or pair of pants) will eliminate triggers that set you up to feel bad about your body.

Don't Put Your Life on Hold

Many people put their life on hold because of their body. For example, some people might hold off buying a new outfit or joining a singles club until they "just lose ten pounds." What are you putting off because of your weight? Complete the Taking Your Life Off Hold Worksheet. Once you have identified the aspects of your life that you have put on hold, you can focus on taking yourself *off* hold by planning on incorporating these activities or events into your life *now*. One strategy that can be helpful is to behave *as if* you were the weight you want to be.

Taking Your Life Off Hold Worksheet

What are you putting off because of your weight? Take a few minutes to examine the events, relationships, or activities you are missing out on because you are waiting for weight loss or because you are unhappy with your body. Record your answers under the categories below.

Self-care (buying a new outfit, going to the salon):

_____

_____

_____

Relationships and social events (taking a vacation, meeting new people, going to a party):

_____

_____

_____

Leisure activities (joining a recreational team, going swimming, learning a new skill):

_____

_____

_____

Are there any other things that you are missing out on?

_____

_____

_____

Make Your Environment Body Friendly

Make your environment a safe place. Get rid of pictures on the refrigerator, diet products, magnets, diet cookbooks, full-length mirrors, and other things that trigger body image concerns.

Avoid Media Triggers

Buy a home décor magazine rather than a fashion magazine and choose television shows that do not trigger body image concerns. Every time Gail watched a popular sitcom with three very skinny and beautiful women on it, she felt fat, ugly, and bad about herself. She felt even worse if her boyfriend watched with her.

Of course it is not possible to avoid all media triggers, so when you are confronted by images that activate negative feelings about your body, examine the images with a critical eye. Remind yourself that almost all of the beauty images in magazines have been altered in some way to make the person appear slimmer, taller, and less wrinkled. These are not realistic images. If in doubt, go stand on any street corner in any city and watch the people go by. Rarely does anyone look like they stepped out of a magazine.

Stop Weighing Yourself

As we've discussed, your bathroom scale can function like an emotional barometer. The scale is also a way to feel in control. For example, Neda weighed herself frequently throughout the day, every day, as a means of checking in with herself to see how she was doing. The scale was Neda's measure of her self-worth and served to fuel her eating disorder and preoccupation with weight and shape. The first few weeks that Neda stopped weighing herself were very difficult. She felt out of control and had increased urges to restrict her eating because she had no measure of her weight. However, it was at this point that Neda could really examine the importance of weighing herself and the role that it played in her body image.

What Role Does the Scale Play for You?

Do not weigh yourself for the next week. You may need to hide the scale, throw it out, or lock it in the trunk of your car. Record the thoughts and feelings that come up as you learn to manage without checking your weight.

Why is it important to weigh yourself?

_____

_____

_____

_____

What are the negatives to not weighing?

_____

_____

_____

_____

What are the positives to not weighing?

_____

_____

_____

_____

Stop Checking Behaviors

In addition to using the scale to check your weight, you may also repeatedly check your appearance in the mirror or check parts of your body with your hands or a tape measure. These checking behaviors increase your focus on your body. As you work on developing a healthier relationship with your body, it is important to eliminate these checking behaviors. What repeated checking behaviors do you need to work on?

_____ Checking your weight on the scale

_____ Checking your appearance in the mirror

_____ Checking the size of parts of your body using your hands or a tape measure

_____ Checking the size of parts of your body using specific clothing or a belt

_____ Checking with others for reassurance

_____ Other _____

Eliminate Negative Body Talk

Monitor your self-talk. When you catch yourself making negative comments to yourself about your body, take a step back and examine the comments you are making. Would you say these comments to a friend? If not, why are you saying them to yourself? Are these comments true? Are these comments helpful? What effect do these comments have on your self-esteem? What is a more neutral or accurate way of capturing how you are feeling? Examine the connection between what you say to yourself and how you feel. Practice counteracting negative self-talk so that it is more neutral.

Rework Your Personal Dictionary

In addition to trying to shift your negative self-talk so that it is more neutral, you can also pay attention to the actual words that you use to describe yourself and your body. Watch out for extreme thinking, where you are categorizing yourself in black-and-white terms: for example, you are fat if you don't feel thin. Try to use more careful and accurate language to describe yourself and substitute neutral words for your shape and weight. For example, "I may not be as thin as most models, but my weight falls in the average range"; "although I am accustomed to feeling fat, that does not mean I am fat"; and "the fattest part of me is my feelings."

Coping with Stereotypes and Prejudice

As much as you may try to work on your body image and shift negative thoughts, there may be factors that work against you. If you are heavier than average, you may be a target of prejudice, bias, and stereotypes perpetuated by our thin-obsessed culture. The problem is *not* with you. It is with our society. Consider the following example. Samantha was monitoring body image thoughts and noticed that every week at her team meeting at work; she would "feel fat" and "disgusting." When we looked more closely at the situation and what was prompting these thoughts and feelings, Samantha reported that the trigger for her was the chairs at the meeting table. She had to sit in a chair with armrests that her body didn't quite fit into. This triggered the thoughts: "I am too big for this chair. I am too fat and I need to lose weight. I feel disgusting." Samantha's interpretation was that there was something wrong with her because she didn't fit comfortably in the chair. The real problem, however, is that companies build chairs to fit an average body size and do not take into account that there are people with a range of body sizes. By shifting her interpretation, Samantha felt better about herself.

Here is another example. Ruby was doing some clothes shopping and saw a pair of pants she really wanted to try on. She was having trouble finding her size on the rack when she noticed the mannequin was also wearing the same pair of pants. When Ruby asked the salesperson if she could check to see the size on the mannequin, the salesperson exclaimed, "There's no point in checking the mannequin because our mannequins don't wear *big* sizes." Immediately, Ruby felt that her body was inadequate and that there was something wrong with her.

What is the problem in this scenario? Is it Ruby's body or the salesperson's thoughtless comment?

Think of a time when something happened that led you to feel bad about your body. Describe the situation below.

_____

_____

_____

_____

What was your interpretation of the situation at the time?

_____

_____

_____

_____

Is there another way to interpret the situation?

_____

_____

_____

_____

Reconnecting with Your Body

So far, we have focused on decreasing your negative body image. In the last part of this chapter, we will focus on developing a more neutral or positive body image. The following exercises and strategies are geared to help you reconnect with your body in ways that are not based on weight, shape, and appearance. Keep an open mind and try each of the exercises and strategies to see what works for you.

What Does Your Body Do for You?

We usually take for granted all of the things our bodies do for us, until something goes wrong. For example, you wake up with a kink in your neck and can't move your head to the side for a few days. It is only now that you think about how easy things are when your body works smoothly. Take a few minutes to consider all of the things your body does for you, in terms of how you function on a daily basis. Make a list below of all of the positive roles your body plays that you may have taken for granted.

_____

_____

_____

_____

If you get stuck, think of the following areas: movement, running your bodily functions, having life, giving life, creativity, imagination, energy, and so on. The next time you find yourself focusing on negative body image, remember the other roles your body plays in your life.

What If Your Body Had Feelings Too?

If your body could talk, what would it tell you? Consider how you have treated your body over the years, both physically and emotionally. Take some time to consider what your body would say. In the space below, record what your body wants to tell you about how it feels.

_____

_____

_____

_____

What is your reaction to what you have written above?

_____

_____

_____

_____

Develop a New Skill

Part of reconnecting with your body is to appreciate its different aspects, apart from shape and weight. One way to do this is to develop a new skill that involves your body in some way. Some people take yoga and find that this is a very powerful method to develop a new awareness of their body in terms of breathing, strength, and balance. Other people may take dancing lessons and develop a new awareness of how their body moves. What skill do you want to learn with your body? Check off the options that interest you below.

___ yoga	___ dance lessons	___ knitting
___ scuba diving	___ meditation	___ martial arts
___ Tai Chi	___ massage	___ art (painting, drawing, etc.)
___ pottery	___ golf	___ skiing
___ bowling	___ volleyball	___ tennis

___ other _____

Checking Your Progress

Earlier in the chapter, you rated both your negative and positive feelings about your body. After you have practiced these new strategies to improve your body image and done these exercises for a few weeks, it is a good idea to check in with your progress.

Negative Body Feelings

Over the past week, how negative have you felt about your body? Rate your general level of negative feelings from 0 to 100, where 0 means you feel neutral (no negative feelings toward your body at all) and 100 means you absolutely despise your body.

0————————————————————————————100
Feel neutral toward   Absolutely despise
your body   your body

Your level of negative body feelings (0–100) ___

Positive Body Feelings

Over the past week, how positive have you felt about your body? Rate your general level of positive feelings from 0 to 100, where 0 means you feel neutral (no positive feelings toward your body at all) and 100 means you feel very positive and comfortable with your body.

0———————————————————————————————100

Feel neutral toward   Very positive and comfortable
     your body   with your body

Your level of positive body feelings (0–100) _____

How do your current ratings about your body compare to the ratings you made earlier? Has there been some progress? Don't be discouraged if you do not see a big difference in your ratings. When you think about how many years it has taken to develop a negative relationship with your body, it is not realistic to think that your feelings will change overnight. Rather, it will take time, patience, and most importantly practice! Developing a healthy relationship with your body takes active strategies that you implement on a daily basis in your life.

Chapter 8

Tackling Underlying Issues

Now that you have worked on your eating, bulimic symptoms, and body image, it is time to address the self-esteem deficits and other issues that underlie your eating disorder. It is important to explore your thoughts and feelings about yourself, your family, relationships, the world, past trauma, and anything else that may have played a role in the development of your bulimia.

Improving Your Sense of Self-Worth

Almost everyone who suffers from bulimia engages in weight-related self-evaluation. In fact, this is a defining characteristic of bulimia and most eating disorders. Weight-related self-evaluation leads to and maintains very low self-esteem in general. Low self-esteem contributes to depression, anxiety, isolation, lack of confidence, and a host of other problems, including bulimia. The goal here is to help you to separate your self-esteem from your weight and shape, and to increase your overall sense of self-worth.

Identifying and Shifting Thoughts

First of all, it is important to identify and challenge the thoughts that you have that foster weight-related self-esteem. What beliefs do you have that encourage you to evaluate yourself based on your weight and shape? You might believe, for example, that being thin means that you are hardworking, likable, successful, strong, or that others will respect you. On the other hand, you might believe that being fat (or not thin) means that you are lazy, unlikable, clumsy, or weak. You can use the Shifting Problematic Thoughts Worksheet from chapter 6 and the exercises described in chapter 7 on body image to try to challenge the connections you make between weight and shape and your self-worth.

It may also be helpful to look at your weight-based self-esteem thoughts from a different perspective. What would you say to your sister/daughter/best friend if she believed that she was only worthwhile if she maintained a certain weight or looked a certain way? Try the following exercise. Think about a person in your life who you love and care about very much. Imagine that the following statements just came out of his or her mouth and then fill in the blanks with what you would say to your loved one in response to these statements.

Your loved one says, "I can't go out tonight because I have gained weight and everyone will notice."

You respond: _____

_____

_____

Your loved one says, "I can't lose weight. I am worthless."

You respond: _____

_____

_____

Your loved one says, "I don't deserve to be happy at this weight. I shouldn't eat."

You respond: _____

_____

_____

Projecting into the Future

You might find your beliefs about weight and shape are very difficult to challenge because they are the rules that you have lived by for some time, and they are constantly reinforced by our society. If this is the case for you, it might be helpful to project into the future and think about how basing your self-esteem on your weight and shape will fit into your life.

Imagine yourself five years from now. How old will you be? What will your life be like if you continue to base your self-esteem on your weight?

_____

_____

_____

_____

_____

Now imagine yourself in ten years' time. How old will you be? What will your life be like if you continue to base your self-esteem on your weight?

_____

_____

_____

_____

_____

How do the descriptions of your life in five and ten years fit in with your values, goals, and aspirations for yourself?

_____

_____

_____

_____

_____

Projecting into the future helps to raise your awareness about your goals and priorities. Although your weight and shape may seem crucially important now, it is usually hard to imagine a lifetime of preoccupation with your body. There are too many things to miss out on if weight and shape continue to be a top priority. Another, more morbid way to make this point is to imagine what you would want written on your headstone after you are gone. To illustrate this, take a look at the following two examples.

RIP

SALLY SMITH
*Sally was a caring
mother of two
wonderful children,
an avid golfer, and
a great coworker,
and a friend to many.
We will miss her.*

RIP

SALLY SMITH
*Sally cared a great
deal about her body.
She weighed herself
daily, and was an
avid dieter and
exerciser. We will
miss her.*

Decisional Balance

Sometimes when your beliefs remain fixed, despite your efforts to modify them, it is useful to examine the usefulness of the belief. To what extent is it useful for you to hold a belief that equates your self-worth with your weight and shape? There may be short- and long-term benefits and costs for continuing with weight-related self-evaluation and for working towards separating your self-worth from your weight and shape. You can weigh the costs and benefits of using this method of self-evaluation by completing the following Decisional Balance Worksheet. (An example is provided.) If you determine that the costs outweigh the benefits, then you can start to let go of this way of evaluating yourself.

Decisional Balance Worksheet Example

	Benefits		Costs	
	Short term	Long term	Short term	Long term
Continuing to evaluate your worth based on your weight and shape	I always have something to do and think about. Keeps me on top of my weight. The scale is a quick and easy way to check if I am okay. Feels familiar and comfortable.	Helps to maintain my weight. Gives me an identity: others know that I care about my weight. Gives me something to do with my life.	I end up feeling badly about myself and depressed. I am obsessed with my weight and shape. I don't have time or energy for other pursuits like socializing and traveling.	Feeling lonely and miserable. Being one-dimensional and uninteresting.
Separating your worth from your weight and shape	I will be able to pursue other interests. May reconnect with friends. Can focus on my career. I will not be obsessed with weight and shape.	Freedom from the scale. Feel better about myself. My life will be more in tune with my values and goals.	I will have nothing to do. Boredom.	Worry that I will gain weight. Lose my identity. Not succeed at anything.

Decisional Balance Worksheet

	Benefits		Costs	
	Short term	Long term	Short term	Long term
Continuing to evaluate your worth based on your weight/shape				
Separating your worth from your weight/shape				

Reconnecting, Reintroducing, and Trying New Things

Another way to start to separate your self-esteem from your weight and shape is to remind yourself of other areas from which you can obtain self-esteem. If you think back to your self-esteem worksheet from chapter 1, these areas may include, but are not limited to, personality, volunteer work, creativity, relationships, athletic ability, artistic ability, spirituality, performance at work or school, talents, hobbies, roles, competence, and knowledge in certain areas. One way to remind yourself of these possibilities is to generate a list of past and current achievements, activities, and roles that have contributed to your self-esteem. Take time now to generate this list.

Past Achievements

_____   _____
_____   _____

Current Achievements

_____   _____
_____   _____

Past Activities

_____   _____
_____   _____

Current Activities

_____   _____
_____   _____

Past Roles

_____   _____
_____   _____

Current Roles

_____   _____
_____   _____

It is not uncommon for an eating disorder to take over your life. Therefore, if you have been struggling with bulimia for a significant amount of time, do not be surprised if you had difficulty generating a list. Alternatively, you may have lots on your list but have lost contact with these areas because of your eating disorder. Look over your list and try to identify what you can reintroduce back into your life. For example, you may have a good friend who you have not spoken to for a long time. You may have enjoyed taking photographs or playing a decent game of volleyball. There may be more current activities or roles that you would like to spend more time cultivating, such as being a good mother or exploring your spirituality. You may have some new interests that you would like to pursue. In order to separate your self-esteem from your weight and shape, it is important to engage in different behaviors and activities.

A word of warning: this is no easy task. For example, Nancy had worked hard to normalize her eating and stop bingeing and vomiting. Her recovery included weight gain, and Nancy was working on separating her self-worth from her weight and shape. This was particularly hard because she had recently retired from a successful career in competitive figure skating, a sport that she excelled at and was involved in from a very young age. Her training schedule had been rigorous and it had not allowed for socializing or many other activities.

Without her skating and her eating disorder, Nancy was feeling lost and worthless. Every time she thought about reconnecting with people or trying new things, she would literally have to force herself to follow through. Forcing the behavior felt wrong, but what Nancy described is a normal and expected feeling during this type of work. It is okay, and even recommended, to make that call or to get involved in an activity, even when you don't feel like doing it. The idea is that once you are involved, your confidence and your self-esteem will grow. Once you are feeling better about yourself, it will get easier to connect with people, and to try new activities.

In terms of your own work of building your self-esteem and separating your weight and shape from your self-worth, what are some activities that you can do? Are there certain people that you would like to reconnect with? If so, you could start by making a phone call or sending a letter or an e-mail. Maybe you are interested in meeting new people. You can join a cooking class, take your dog to a nearby dog park, or sign up for a camping trip or a dating service. Take some time now to think about what you can add to your life that is unrelated to your appearance and complete the following worksheet.

Reconnecting, Reintroducing, and Trying-New-Things Worksheet

Spend some time brainstorming, and list anything that you could do to help build your self-esteem in areas other than weight and shape. Include activities, hobbies, interests, and people that you might like to contact.

Activities

_____   _____

_____   _____

_____   _____

Hobbies

_____   _____

_____   _____

_____   _____

Interests

_____   _____

_____   _____

_____   _____

People to Contact

_____   _____

_____   _____

_____   _____

List five realistic goals that you can accomplish within the next two weeks (e.g., e-mail Susie, pick up a home-decorating magazine, schedule some time to go horseback riding, go to a foreign film, make a call about taking some classes, update your resume).

1. _____

2. _____

3. _____

4. _____

5. _____

Modifying Perfectionism

Perfectionism is a personality trait that plays a role in the development and maintenance of bulimia nervosa (Fairburn et al. 1997). In fact, bulimia nervosa may be viewed as a direct expression of perfectionism because of the drive to perfect your body (Shafran, Cooper, and Fairburn 2002). Perfectionism is a drive to obtain excellence. In many cases, perfectionism can be healthy, motivating, and functional. This type of healthy perfectionism has been referred to as *positive perfectionism* (Frost et al. 1993). However, in many cases, and specifically with respect to bulimia, perfectionism can be unhealthy and lead to negative consequences to the self. This type of unhealthy perfectionism has been referred to as *clinical perfectionism* (Shafran, Cooper, and Fairburn 2002) or *dysfunctional perfectionism* (Frost et al. 1993). Unhealthy perfectionism includes the following characteristics (Hamachek 1978):

* never seeing your efforts as good enough

* always thinking that you should have done better

* interpreting self-satisfaction and self-content as signs of laziness and weakness

* preoccupation with doing things just right

* always trying to do better than you have done in the past

* setting self-imposed high standards that are impossible and unreasonable to obtain

* a high degree of self-criticism when attempts to meet impossible goals are met with failure

* overvaluing achievement

* undervaluing self-worth

* selectively focusing on what is wrong (failures) and ignoring positive aspects (successes)

* evaluating yourself based on achievement, rather than just being yourself

When you have bulimia, your perfectionism is focused on the area of weight, shape, and eating. You may also have perfectionistic tendencies in other areas of your life (for example, school, career, relationships, athletic ability). You may set goals for yourself that are unrealistic and impossible to achieve. These high standards set you up for failure, which results in self-criticism and erosion of your self-worth.

Strategies for Modifying Perfectionism

Try the following strategies to modify your perfectionism. These strategies are based on work by Shafran, Cooper, and Fairburn (2002).

Increase Your Awareness

Examine the role that perfectionism plays in your life. Take some time now to think about where your perfectionism is focused and what impact it has had on you by answering the following questions:

What role does perfectionism play in your life?

_____

_____

_____

What impact does your perfectionism have on your self-worth?

_____

_____

_____

In what ways do you express your perfectionism that is unhealthy or unhelpful for you?

_____

_____

_____

Are there any healthy or positive aspects to your perfectionism?

_____

_____

_____

What factors led to the development of your perfectionism (family, childhood, life experiences)?

_____

_____

_____

In what way is your perfectionism a problem for you?

_____

_____

_____

Develop Alternatives

Develop new ways to evaluate yourself other than your achievement. You can expand the domains that you base your self-worth on by following the same strategies you use to challenge your weight-related self-evaluation.

Conduct Behavior Experiments

Compare how you feel about yourself when you are following your perfectionistic standards to how you feel when you purposely don't follow them. For example, Min always felt good about herself when she would restrict her breakfast and lunch. In therapy, Min and her therapist came up with a behavioral experiment for her to try. She would purposely break her eating rule by making a date with a friend to go out to lunch and eat whatever her friend ate. Min found that although she felt bad that she ate more than she would have liked, she also felt good about herself for reconnecting with her friend.

Cathy always liked to have everything neat and tidy and impeccably clean. She would never invite someone over to her house unless she spent a few hours cleaning. For her behavioral experiment, Cathy invited some friends over and didn't spend any time cleaning the house beforehand. Although she felt anxious when her friends were over, she realized that they didn't notice that she hadn't cleaned at all. In fact, they acted just the same as they did when she had spent hours cleaning in advance. She realized that her friends' opinions of her didn't really change based on how clean her house was.

What behavioral experiments can you try? Think about things that you can do that will deliberately break your perfectionistic standards and then compare the outcome to when you follow the old rules. Complete the following worksheet each time you conduct a behavioral experiment. Make plenty of copies.

Behavioral Experiment Worksheet

List a perfectionistic rule or standard that you generally follow:

_____

Plan an activity that you can do that deliberately breaks your perfectionistic rule:

_____

Once you have completed the activity, compare the outcome to what happens when you follow your perfectionistic rule. What are the differences (your reaction, the reaction of others, how it turns out, how you feel)?

_____

_____

_____

What have you learned from this behavioral experiment?

_____

_____

_____

What will you try next?

_____

Shift Your Perfectionistic Thoughts

Identify distortions in your thoughts. Are you focusing on your failures and ignoring your successes? Would you expect anyone else to live up to the standards that you set? Are you narrowing your focus on one area (weight, shape, eating, career, school, athletic performance) and ignoring other aspects of yourself (personality, relationships, sense of humor)? What would be a more realistic view? Complete the following worksheet to practice modifying your perfectionistic thoughts and attitudes.

Shifting Perfectionistic Thoughts Worksheet

Over the next week, use this sheet to monitor your perfectionistic thoughts and counteract unrealistic standards and attitudes. Complete this form whenever you notice that you are experiencing a downward shift in how you are feeling about yourself. Record what feelings you are experiencing and the intensity of each feeling from 0 (not at all) to 100 (most extreme). Record the situation or trigger associated with the feeling(s). Record any thoughts that were going through your mind at the time. Examine the thoughts for any distortions. Counteract the distortions. Rerate your feelings (0 to 100) and then record the outcome or how you responded to the situation or trigger.

Feeling(s) and Urges Rate (0–100)	Situation or Trigger	Perfectionistic Standards, Beliefs, Rules, and Attitudes	Realistic View (How would someone without an eating disorder think about this situation? Are you focusing on your failures and ignoring your successes? Are you applying a double standard to yourself in that you would never expect anyone else to live up to the standards that you set? Are you narrowing your focus on one area and ignoring other aspects of yourself? How useful is this way of thinking?)	Rerate Feelings (0–100)	Outcome

Working through Past Trauma

Your eating disorder may serve as a protection from past traumatic experiences. The eating disorder may distract your mind from painful events from the past, mask powerful emotions, or numb your feelings. For example, Sela had been sexually abused by a relative when she was a teenager. When she told her parents about the assault, they cut off contact with that side of the family. They did not let the police know, and they also did not discuss the incident again. It became an unspoken secret. Shortly after, Sela developed bulimia. Her struggle with bulimia and her preoccupation with her weight, shape, and eating consumed all of her mental energy. She no longer thought about the past abuse, and she buried her feelings about the events. Years later, Sela went for treatment for her bulimia. As she recovered and got her eating disorder symptoms under control, the memories of the past abuse resurfaced along with painful and overwhelming emotions. At this point, Sela realized that her eating disorder had served to help her keep the past in the past. Once Sela started to process the events of the past in therapy, she realized that, for her, feeling fat was not really about weight. Rather, when she felt fat or "dirty," she was really feeling ashamed about the sexual abuse.

If you suffered from trauma or abuse, part of recovery from your eating disorder may mean having to work through these events from the past. The strategies that you have learned in this book should be helpful. However, this may not be enough. If you find that you are having repeated thoughts of past events that pop into your head when you don't want or expect them to, or if you are having nightmares about a past event, or if you sometimes feel like you are reliving a past event, you should seek professional help. A supportive therapist will be able to help you manage your post-traumatic symptoms and work through your past trauma. Refer to chapter 13 for information on how to find professional help.

Strategies for Working through Past Trauma

The most important strategy for working through past trauma is to process the powerful emotions associated with the event(s). Emotions that you may be dealing with include feelings of guilt and shame. You may feel worthless, used, inadequate, ashamed, guilty, violated, and betrayed. Note: "feeling dirty" may represent a number of painful feelings.

If you suffered from past trauma or abuse, label your feelings about it below. Try to be specific.

_____

_____

_____

_____

Examine the thoughts that you have associated with your feelings. Are they accurate? Are there distortions? Some people think that they should have been able to stop it. This is like blaming the victim. In most cases, trauma is perpetrated by a powerful person on someone who is vulnerable, holds less power, or who is helpless in being able to stop the abuse. So realistically, you didn't have the ability to stop it or you would have. You may have the belief that you are "bad" because bad things happened to you. It is important to remember that a bad thing happened to you and that doesn't mean that you are a bad person. In fact, it is the perpetrator who is responsible for the abusive behavior. Sometimes people do feel sexual pleasure even when the sexual activity is unwanted or abusive. For some people, this mixture of pleasure in with the horror of the event can lead to feelings of guilt and shame. Feeling aroused is a biological state that results from stimulation; it does not mean that you enjoyed being abused or wanted it to happen.

You can use the technique of shifting your problematic thoughts to work through the thoughts that you have associated with your feelings and the past trauma. You can also use relaxation strategies (see mindfulness exercise in chapter 5) to help manage your distress when you are feeling overwhelmed or anxious.

Identifying and Coping with Emotions

Many people with bulimia talk about how their eating disorder is a way to prevent or cope with emotions. Bingeing may provide you with comfort, distract you from emotions, or the guilt associated with bingeing may mask more threatening feelings of loneliness and unworthiness. Vomiting or exercising may relieve anxiety and tension. Restricting or keeping your weight below its set point can make you feel numb and emotionless. Also, some people communicate their emotions to other people through symptoms. For example, whenever Julie was angry with her husband, she responded by refusing food. This was one way to get her husband's attention and not have to communicate her anger directly.

As you work to stop your bulimic symptoms, it is likely that emotions may start to surface for you. This may be a foreign experience for you and you may feel totally overwhelmed. For example, Lori, who was not used to feeling emotions, described this process as feeling like butterflies in her stomach. Another person described it as feeling like he had snakes crawling all over his body. You may have received messages in your life that led you to believe that your emotions were incorrect, invalid, wrong, or selfish. You may not have been taught adaptive skills to identify and express your emotions. Alternatively, your family may have been chaotic and emotional but dealt with emotions using violence or other maladaptive methods. As a result, you may have been using your eating disorder to avoid or cope with your feelings. The first step to getting in touch with your emotions is to identify them, and the second step is to learn more adaptive ways of expressing and coping with them. The next section of this chapter is based on the work of Edmund Bourne (2000).

Facts about Feelings

To begin with, feelings are not right or wrong. A feeling is a feeling, and if you feel it, then it exists. Sometimes the thoughts that lead up to a feeling may be unrealistic or invalid, but the feeling itself should not be judged.

Feelings can involve a complete body reaction including your brain and your autonomic nervous system. If you are anxious, you may also experience a racing heart and sweaty palms, angry feelings may include tension in your neck or shaking of your body, and sadness can lead to a loss of energy and appetite.

Some feelings may be easier to identify because they occur in a pure form such as fear, anger, or sadness. Other feelings are more complex and involve thoughts and evaluations, such as feeling ineffective, lonely, or worthless. Also, you may experience a mixture of feelings, such as sadness, guilt, and anger in response to the death of a loved one or fear, sadness, and excitement in the face of recovery. In these cases, it is important to sort out your feelings by identifying and processing each of the feelings involved. Sometimes you may also feel one emotion instead of another perhaps more powerful or threatening emotion.

Sometimes it makes sense to ignore feelings in your day-to-day living. For example, if you are feeling angry toward your partner from an argument in the morning, you may need to put those feelings aside to function properly at work. However, ignored and suppressed feelings can build up over time. If not properly addressed, they can either be let out uncontrollably during times of stress or leave you feeling anxious, empty, or numb. If you are in touch with your feelings, you are likely to feel more energetic and grounded in the long run.

Identifying Emotions

It is important to try to identify the exact feeling that you are experiencing. As you try to identify your feelings, remember that "fat" and "bingey" are not feelings. The best way to identify feelings is to try to tune into your body. Focusing on your thoughts and worries tends to keep you out of touch with your feelings. In order to gain access to your feelings it is important to try to quiet these thoughts and allow yourself to scan your body. This does not mean to focus on how much you dislike your body, but rather to become aware of your internal sensations that may give you clues to what emotions you might be feeling. For example, tension in your body may be indicative of anger, jittery sensations may be a sign of frustration or fear, and headaches and nausea may represent feelings of shame or hopelessness.

You can use the following lists of positive and negative feelings to help you describe your own.

Positive Feelings

accepted
adventurous
affectionate
alive
amazed
ambitious
amused
beautiful
brave
calm
capable
caring
cheerful
cherished
comfortable
competent
composed
confident
courageous
curious
delighted
desirable
determined
eager
ecstatic

elated
energetic
enthusiastic
euphoric
excited
exhilarated
forgiving
friendly
fulfilled
generous
glad
good
grateful
great
happy
hopeful
humorous
important
inspired
joyful
jubilant
lovable
loved
loving
loyal

motivated
nostalgic
nurtured
optimistic
overjoyed
passionate
peaceful
playful
pleased
proud
relaxed
relieved
respected
safe
satisfied
secure
self-reliant
silly
special
strong
supportive
sympathetic
tender
triumphant
trusting
worthy

Negative Feelings

abandoned
admonished
afraid
aggravated
agitated
alone
angry
anguished
anxious
appalled
apprehensive
ashamed
awkward
baffled
bewildered
bitter
bored
chastised
confused
contempt
crusty
deadened
defeated
degraded
dejected
dependent
depressed
despairing
desperate
destroyed
devastated
disappointed
discouraged
disgusted
disheartened
dismal
distraught
distrustful
disturbed
embarrassed

empty
enraged
exasperated
excluded
exposed
failed
fearful
filthy
foolish
frantic
frenzied
frightened
frustrated
furious
futile
guilty
hateful
helpless
hollow
hopeless
horrified
hostile
humiliated
hurt
hysterical
ignored
impatient
inadequate
incompetent
inconsolable
incurable
indecisive
ineffective
inferior
inhibited
insecure
insufficient
inundated
irritated
isolated

jealous
loathsome
lonely
lost
melancholy
miserable
misunderstood
muddled
needy
numb
obligated
outraged
overwhelmed
overwrought
panicky
pathetic
pessimistic
repulsed
scared
stressed
tense
terrified
thwarted
tormented
touchy
trapped
troubled
unappreciated
unattractive
uncertain
uncomfortable
uneasy
unfulfilled
unpleasant
unworthy
upset
uptight
vulnerable
woeful
worried

In his *Anxiety and Phobia Workbook*, Edmund Bourne (2000) describes five steps to help you tune into your body based on Eugene Gendlin's (1978) focusing technique. Follow the steps below the next time that you have urges for symptoms or the next time you are feeling upset, tense, "fat," "dirty," emotionally numb, or just generally confused about how you are feeling.

1. Physically Relax. Try to slow yourself down. Do something that you know physically relaxes you. Take a bath, read, or listen to music. Or, try deep breathing for five minutes. Breathe in and out through your nose. Breathe from your diaphragm and try to lengthen and slow your breathing. Your stomach should distend as you exhale (not your chest). Try imagining a pleasant nature scene that is meaningful to you, such as a ducks swimming on a lake or a wind blowing through your favorite garden or park, as you continue to breathe.

2. Ask yourself, "what am I feeling right now?" or "what is my main concern right now?"

3. Tune into that place in your body where you feel emotional sensations. Often this will be in the area of your heart or your stomach.

4. Wait and listen to whatever you can sense or pick up on. Don't try to analyze or judge what's there. Be an observer and allow yourself to sense any feelings that are waiting to surface. Simply wait until something emerges.

5. If you are still having trouble identifying your feelings, return to step 1 and try some more relaxation techniques.

Tolerating Emotions

Once you have started to identify your feelings, it is important to learn how to tolerate them. It is okay to sit with your feelings. You do not have to use symptoms to numb or distract yourself. Feelings, at first, may seem uncomfortable, unbearable, or even torturous, but remember that nothing drastic is going to happen if you allow yourself to feel the feelings. If you are frightened of your feelings, it might be helpful to examine your thoughts about feelings. For example, Ingrid believed that if she allowed herself to feel her feelings of sadness, she would be overwhelmed and something terrible would happen. When questioned further about this, she was able to articulate that she feared that she would "freak out" and that her "head would explode." Further questioning helped her identify that "freaking out" meant that she would cry, sob, and her nose would run. Although this emotional reaction is very unpleasant and embarrassing for Ingrid, it is a big jump from her head exploding. Once Ingrid realized that the worst-case scenario was not so bad, she was able to tolerate her feelings of sadness and learn to express those feelings.

Expressing Emotions

There are a variety of different ways to express and process emotions. You may want to try different techniques depending on the emotion and the situation.

Talking to someone supportive. A supportive person is someone who can listen to how you are feeling, validate your emotions, and maybe help you sort out your feelings. Ideally this person is not closely connected to the situation that may have led to the negative feelings. If you have someone like this in your life, reach out to them and talk to them when you are feeling badly. Possibilities include partners, family members, friends, supervisors, coworkers, church members, doctors, therapists, and support groups.

Communicating your feelings to the source. It is also okay and often beneficial to talk directly to the individual, if there is an individual involved, whose actions may have led to your negative feelings. However, it is important that this person is willing to hear you out. Not everyone will be. Usually it is best to take some time and try to sort out your feelings before going to the source. It is also best to try to frame your concerns so as not to come across like you are attacking or criticizing the person, so that you can avoid a defensive reaction. State the facts, and then try to focus on how you are feeling. For example, you can communicate your feelings by saying, "When you don't call when you say you are going to, it makes me feel abandoned and unloved," or "When you ignore my requests, I end up feeling disrespected and angry," or "When you criticize my choices, I feel ineffective and sad."

Writing about feelings. Writing may be a good alternative even if you have someone to talk to. There is something about writing in a private journal that helps to process emotions that may be more difficult to talk about. This is also a good option if you wish to process emotions related to another person who is not available (not willing, not capable, dead, ill, or distant) to speak with you. Also, it can be helpful to write a letter to another person that expresses your emotions. You can always decide later whether you want to deliver the letter or not. In some cases, delivering the letter is not an option, but just writing everything down may help you to express certain feelings. For example, Adelia had tons of feelings after her best friend completed suicide. After some time of trying to deal with her emotions without success (bingeing and trying not to think about her friend), she decided to write her friend a letter to try to express the feelings of anger, sadness, confusion, and guilt that she was experiencing due to the suicide. Although this was an extremely difficult thing to do, Adelia felt like she had said what she needed to say to her friend in the letter, and in the end she felt some relief.

Crying. Sometimes a good cry can help to process emotions. If you find that you have difficulty crying or getting in touch with your own sadness, it can be helpful to watch a sad movie or listen to sad music to help you get started.

Creative expression. Some people process emotions through creative expression. This includes composing music, writing poetry, drawing, painting, sculpting, and acting. If you are already involved in any of these arts, or if any of them interest you, it is worthwhile to test them out.

Examining Your Core Beliefs

As you work on developing alternative ways of thinking, you may wonder why old thoughts keep coming up again and again. The reason is that these thoughts are fueled by a deeper set of beliefs, your core beliefs. *Core beliefs* are the fundamental beliefs that you have of yourself, others, and the world around you, and your future, that have developed through your experiences in childhood and throughout your life (Beck 1995). Unlike thoughts that run through your head and are generally quite easy to identify, you may not be aware of the core beliefs that you hold. Core beliefs are absolute, global statements about yourself, others, and the future—for example: "I am worthless," "others are critical," and "the future is bleak." Just like you have learned to shift your negative thoughts, you can also learn to modify your core beliefs. The goal is for your core beliefs to be less absolute, more flexible, and more realistic. Consider the following examples:

Negative Core Beliefs	Modified Core Belief
I am worthless.	I am a worthwhile person and have positive and negative aspects like everyone else.
I am insufficient.	I am sufficient and can only do my best, which is good enough.
I am weak.	I am a human being with both strengths and weaknesses, and that is okay.
I am unloveable.	I am loved and can give love. Therefore, I am a loving person. I just have trouble giving love to myself.
Others are critical.	Sometimes others are critical, but the majority of people are tolerant, accepting, and caring. The most critical person of me is myself.
The world is uncontrollable.	There are things in this world that are beyond my control, but there are also many things that I can control. I can control how I choose to react to the things life throws my way.
The future is bleak.	The future holds opportunities for me that I am not aware of and may look bleak at times, but there is hope around the next corner.

Identifying Your Core Beliefs

Take some time now to look back at your Thought Monitoring and Shifting Problematic Thoughts Worksheets from chapter 6. See if you have recorded any thoughts that are really core beliefs (absolute, rigid statements about yourself, others, or the world). Use the next worksheet to further uncover your core beliefs.

Identifying Core Beliefs Worksheet

Take some time to think about your deepest thoughts and attitudes about yourself, the view you have of other people and the world around you, and your perception of the future. Complete the sentences below to help you access your core beliefs.

Core beliefs about yourself:

I am _____

I am _____

I am _____

I am _____

I am _____

Core beliefs about other people and the world:

Other people are _____

Other people are _____

Other people are _____

The world is _____

The world is _____

The world is _____

Core beliefs about the future:

The future is _____

The future is _____

The future is _____

The future is _____

Shifting Core Beliefs

It may be easy to tap into your core beliefs, or it may take time and continued monitoring of your thoughts for you to become aware of your core beliefs. Just reading through this section has increased your awareness of the different levels of thoughts that you hold, and this increased awareness should help you to recognize core beliefs that may come up. Once you have identified a problematic core belief, you can work on shifting it. Follow these steps:

Step 1. Identify the core belief. A core belief is different from a problematic thought, in that problematic thoughts are usually specific to situations or triggers and are easier to identify. Core beliefs apply more globally, are rigid and absolute, and are often below immediate awareness.

Step 2. Consider the evidence. What evidence do you have that this core belief is not true? Is there a more flexible and realistic view? Does this belief ring true for all situations?

Step 3. Rewrite your core belief. The shifted core belief should look more balanced, flexible, and less absolute. The goal is to shift the belief to make it more realistic and accurate.

Step 4. Consider where the core belief came from. What experiences have you had that may have led to this belief? Often, understanding what factors may have contributed to the belief makes it easier to shift.

Cary had been working on shifting her problematic thoughts for a few weeks. Her problematic thoughts primarily revolved around "never doing enough" and "having to be perfect." For Cary, a recurring theme was the core belief, "I am not good enough." When she looked for the source of this belief, she realized that when she was growing up, she was never able to make her mother happy. Whatever she did, her mother would point out other things that she could do to improve. From these experiences, Cary had developed the belief that she was not good enough and had spent her life trying to be perfect, in order to compensate for the problem. Once Cary was aware of where her core belief came from, it was easier for her to shift it. She recognized that she had always tried her best, and that was certainly good enough. Use the next worksheet to help shift your core beliefs.

Shifting Core Beliefs Worksheet

Record your core belief in the first column. Rate how much you believe this statement on a scale of 0 to 100, where 0 means you do not believe it at all and 100 means that you believe it completely. In the second column, record any evidence, facts, or experiences you have that are inconsistent with the core belief. Based on the evidence, rewrite your core belief so that it is more accurate, realistic, and flexible. Rate how much you believe the modified core belief on the same scale. Now that you have considered a more balanced view, rerate your belief in the original core belief based on the same scale. Finally, in the last column, record any important factors (experiences from childhood, family, life) that you feel may have led you to form your original core belief.

Core Belief Rate (0–100)	Evidence Core Belief Is Not True	Modified Core Belief Rate (0–100)	Rerate Your Original Belief (0–100)	Factors That Led to Core Belief

Chapter 9

Managing Self-Harm, Impulsive Behavior, and Substance Use

Research has shown that people who have bulimia often struggle with other problems as well, including self-harm behaviors, impulsive or reckless behaviors, substance-use problems, depression, and anxiety (Mitchell et al. 1986). In this chapter, we cover a group of behaviors that involve acting on impulses or urges, including self-harm, impulsive or reckless behaviors, and substance use. Note: If you find that you are hurting yourself, if you feel that you are not able to control impulses for behaviors that are unhealthy for you, or if your substance use is controlling you, you may need to seek additional help. We hope this book will help you focus on these problems.

As you read on, feel free to skip over sections if they cover issues which you are experiencing no difficulty with. If none of this material seems relevant, you can simply move on to the next chapter.

Self-Harm Behaviors

Self-harm behaviors refer to any actions performed to inflict harm or injury to the self. The most common type of self-harm behavior is skin cutting (wrists, arms, stomach, and legs) (Favazza and Conterio 1988). Less common forms of self-harm behavior include burning, picking, interfering with wound healing, hitting, biting, scratching, and hair pulling. These behaviors may affect the arms and hands, face, legs, and, in fewer cases, the genitals. Self-harm behaviors are often done repetitively, without the intention of suicide, and lead to minor or moderate levels of harm. Many people who struggle with bulimia may also engage in self-harm behaviors (Favazza, DeRosear, and Conterio 1989). One study found that 34.3 percent of 137 women with bulimia reported engaging in self-injurious behavior. Those individuals who reported self-harm behaviors were more likely to have experienced past traumatic events; and for about half of the group, the self-harm behaviors began before the eating disorder started (Paul et al. 2002).

Self-harm behaviors may be used for a variety of reasons, including decreasing feelings of dissociation in an attempt to feel more grounded or "real," managing emotional distress, and coping with post-traumatic symptoms (Briere and Gil 1998). Other functions include reducing anger or guilt, punishing the self, reducing tension, translating emotional pain into body pain, and ending uncomfortable feelings (Paul et al. 2002). In fact, self-harm behavior may serve a number of functions simultaneously (Suyemoto 1998). Consider the following example.

Jasmine is twenty-three years old and has been struggling with bulimia since she was in her teens. She first began cutting as a way of punishing herself for the way her body looked. She would cut her arms and the tops of her thighs. Cutting would make her feel like she had done something productive and taken control of the situation. It would also temporarily stop overwhelming feelings of self-hatred and disgust. Jasmine would engage in episodes of self-harm a few times per month. The reasons motivating Jasmine's self-harm changed over time. Jasmine found that during periods when she restricted her eating she felt emotionally numb. She wouldn't feel anything. When her boyfriend shared intimate feelings with her, she felt an emotional distance, and even though she wanted to feel more, she was unable to. In response to this emotional numbness, Jasmine would cut herself so that she would feel something, anything. She described the feeling that she got from cutting as a sign that she was alive and could feel something. For Jasmine, self-harm served a number of functions, including turning off painful emotions, self-punishment, and coping with numbness.

Identifying Triggers

Self-harm behavior can be used as a coping strategy in response to a variety of triggers:

* ✸ Perception of an interpersonal loss (e.g., your friend cancels a date) may trigger self-harm behavior as a way of coping with feelings of abandonment and isolation.

* ✸ Overwhelming emotions such as extreme tension, anxiety, anger, and fear may trigger self-harm behavior, because feelings or sensations resulting

from self-harm distract from overwhelming emotions and, by creating emotional distance, make them more manageable.

✹ Feelings of dissociation or feeling numb or "nothing," may trigger self-harm behaviors in order to feel something and to feel alive, more grounded or "real"; alternatively, self-harm may cause dissociation and provide relief through numbness.

✹ Self-harm behaviors may fulfill a need for self-punishment or a need to express guilt, other emotions, or conflict.

✹ Finally, just as your eating disorder may be a way of feeling in control of your life, self-harm behavior may also be a way of feeling in control (Suyemoto 1998).

Looking at the Consequences

After engaging in self-harm, some people feel an immediate sense of relief or calmness. Others may also feel guilty that they engaged in the behavior or disgusted with themselves. There are also physical consequences from self-harm behaviors, including damage to your body through wounds, scabs, scars, and risk of infection.

What self-harm behavior(s) do you engage in?

_____

_____

_____

How often?

_____

_____

_____

What triggers your urges to self-harm?

_____

_____

_____

_____

What function(s) do self-harm behaviors serve in your life?

_____

_____

_____

_____

_____

What are the consequences of your self-harm behavior(s)?

_____

_____

_____

_____

_____

How does your self-harm behavior fit with your goals for the future and what is important to you?

_____

_____

_____

_____

_____

What other more healthy ways can you use to fulfill the needs or serve the functions of your self-harm behavior(s)?

_____

_____

_____

_____

_____

Strategies for Change

In this section, there are a number of different strategies that you can try to help you eliminate your self-harm behaviors and manage urges to self-harm. It is important to try each strategy to find the ones that work best for you. In addition to using the strategies we discuss below, you may also want to review the coping strategies covered in chapter 5. Many of the strategies you've been practicing to avoid acting on eating disorder symptoms can be applied to urges to self-harm.

Problem Solving

One strategy that has been found to be helpful in reducing self-harm behavior is a technique called *problem solving* (Townsend et al. 2001). This technique is not only useful for dealing with urges to self-harm, it may also be used for any other problems that you are facing. The rationale behind the problem-solving technique is that problems in your life can lead to negative and unpleasant emotions, psychological distress, and even physical symptoms (tension, difficulty sleeping, headaches, and so on). Often you may focus on the effects of the problems in your life (emotional and physical consequences), rather than the problems themselves. By more effectively managing your problems, you will find that you can reduce the emotional and physical consequences.

The problem-solving technique involves the following steps as outlined by Mynors-Wallis and Hegel (2000):

Step 1. Make a problem list. Record all of the problems that you are dealing with in your life. Different areas include your relationships with a partner, relationships with your family members, relationships with friends, finances, health, work/ school, housing, and legal issues.

Step 2. Identify a specific problem to work on. Looking at your list of problems may seem overwhelming, so remind yourself that you will be tackling things one step at a time. Review your list of problems and choose the problem that you would like to work on first. This is often the problem that is bothering you the most.

Step 3. Set a goal. Now set a goal for yourself. If you didn't have this problem, how would your life be different? What would you be doing differently? The answers to these questions will help you to set your goal. You want your goal to be specific. If your goal is vague ("I want to feel better"), it is going to be hard for you to know what to do to achieve the goal. Your goal should also be achievable.

Step 4. Brainstorm. Now that you have a goal, take some time to brainstorm solutions for achieving your goal. Don't judge your solutions. Rather, just record any ideas that you have. You will evaluate each idea in the next step.

Step 5. Choose a solution. Review your list of solutions. Is there a solution that makes sense to try first?

Step 6. Make a plan. Now that you have a solution, you need to make a specific plan of how you are going to carry out your solution. What steps do you need to take to put your plan in place?

Step 7. Implement the plan. Now it is time to put your plan into action.

Step 8. Evaluate the outcome. Once you have implemented your plan, take some time to reflect on the outcome. Have you achieved your goal? Do you need to try a new solution? Did any obstacles come up that you need to plan for? If you have been successful in achieving your goal, you can start to work on another problem, beginning the process at step 2.

We've devised a Problem-Solving Worksheet to help you practice this technique. Some of your problems may be unsolvable (such as the break up of a relationship or a chronic illness). In this case, you can still use the problem-solving technique by focusing on the impact that the unsolvable problem has had on your life and how it is affecting you. The following example illustrates how problem-solving can help you resist urges to self-harm.

Jasmine (who was described earlier in the chapter) had strong urges to self-harm one evening as she was getting ready for bed. Instead of following through on her urges, she took some time to fill in the problem-solving worksheet. When she thought about the things going on in her life, and the events of the day, she realized that she had a lot of problems going on that she hadn't been aware of, which were causing her significant stress. She was planning to move in with her boyfriend, but she was also unsure how she felt about making this commitment. Her boyfriend had recently lost his job. She was unclear about when they would move in together and how they would support themselves. She was feeling some stress at work due to a problem with her boss. She was also experiencing stress at home, as her parents constantly watched whatever she ate. After thinking about all of the things going on in her life, Jasmine had a better awareness of the triggers for her urge to self-harm. She wrote down her problems, as follows:

* unsure about details of moving in with boyfriend

* unsure about the move (concerned about how moving in would affect the relationship)

* concerned about how to afford the move

* stress at work due to conflict with boss

* stress at home due to parents watching eating every moment.

Jasmine decided that the problem that was bothering her most was her uncertainty about how moving in together might affect their relationship. She identified this as the problem that she would work on first. She set her goal as follows: "have a better understanding of my feelings about moving in together by next week." Jasmine's goal was specific; she wanted to understand what feelings she had. She decided to work on this goal over the next week.

The next step in the problem-solving technique is to brainstorm all of the possible solutions for achieving the goal that you have identified. Jasmine brainstormed the following solutions:

* talk to her boyfriend about her feelings

* talk to her best friend about her feelings

* write her feelings down in her journal

Jasmine decided that first she would try writing about her feelings in her journal so that she had a better understanding of what was going on for her. Then she would talk to her boyfriend to share her feelings and get support.

Jessica's plan was as follows:

* Write about my feelings before I go to bed.

* Read over what I wrote tomorrow after work and write more if I feel the need to.

* Call my boyfriend and make a plan for this weekend to talk about our moving in together (plan to go for a walk with the dogs so that we will have time and privacy to talk).

After Jessica implemented the plan, she would evaluate how effective her solutions were for achieving her goal. If she still felt like she hadn't achieved her goal, she planned to try talking to her best friend. After going through the problem-solving worksheet, Jessica felt more positive. She had a better sense of the challenges that she was struggling with, and she felt more positive that she was taking control and tackling the issues. Jessica found that her urge to self-harm had passed and she went to bed feeling better about things.

Problem-Solving Worksheet

1. **Make a problem list.** List the problems that are going on in your life right now:

_____

_____

_____

_____

_____

2. **Identify a specific problem to work on.** Reviewing your list above, what problem do you want to tackle first?

_____

3. **Set a goal.** Set a goal related to this problem. How would you like your life to change? If you didn't have this problem, what would you be doing differently? Make your goal specific and achievable.

_____

4. **Brainstorm.** Record all possible solutions to achieve your goal.

_____

_____

_____

_____

5. **Choose a solution.** Review all possible solutions above and select one to try. If you have difficulty choosing a solution, consider the pros and cons of each one.

_____

_____

_____

_____

6. **Make a plan.** How will you implement your solution? What are the steps you need to take? Be specific.

_____

_____

_____

_____

_____

7. **Implement your plan.** Put your plan into action.

8. **Evaluate the outcome.** How did your plan work out? Did any obstacles arise? Did you achieve your goal?

_____

_____

_____

_____

_____

What is your next step?

_____

_____

Self-Soothing

Overwhelming emotions are often a trigger for self-harm urges, so one strategy for decreasing urges to self-harm is to develop other ways of making yourself feel better, to calm yourself down, comfort yourself, and reduce painful emotions. What thoughts or activities might be self-soothing for you? You might want to think about what advice you would give to a friend who was feeling horrible and looking for a way to feel better. Consider trying the following self-soothing responses.

Self-soothing thoughts. The next time you are feeling really awful and have urges to hurt yourself, try focusing on one of the thoughts below. If you have comforting thoughts that you have used in the past, write them down in the blanks provided, or try to create a new self-soothing thought for yourself.

* These horrible feelings will pass.

* I am a good person.

* It is okay to have strong feelings.

* Just because I feel like a bad person doesn't mean it is true.

* I am strong.

* I can cope with this.

* _____

* _____

Self-soothing behaviors. Doing comforting things may also help alleviate your urges to self-harm. Try one of the suggested behaviors below. If you know of an activity that has comforted you in the past, write it down in the space provided, or try to think of a new self-soothing behavior for yourself and write it here.

* Write about your emotions in your journal.

* Take a bath.

* Spend time with your pet.

* Channel your energy into something creative (draw a picture, write a poem).

* Take a walk and pay attention to the nature around you.

* Call a good friend.

* Watch a funny movie or television show.

* _____

* _____

* _____

Using guided imagery. Another strategy to use for self-soothing is guided imagery. Guided imagery involves focusing on an image associated with comfort and relaxation in your mind and imagining the image as vividly as possible. This technique is usually done with a therapist or someone taking you through the imagery step-by-step while your eyes are closed.

Guided imagery has been found to be an effective technique for improving self-comforting in women with bulimia (Esplen, Gallop, and Garfinkel 1999). You can try using imagery by following the exercise below. Read the exercise out loud into a tape recorder. Try to read the exercise slowly and in a calm and soothing voice. Then you can just sit back and relax and listen to the tape to guide you whenever you like.

Find a quiet place and get comfortable. Close your eyes. Now turn your attention to your breathing. With each breath in, the cleansing air is calming your spirits. With each breath out, your stress and tension are released. Breathe in slowly, one, two, three. Breathe out slowly, one, two, three. And in—one, two, three. And out—one, two, three. As you continue to breathe, your breathing becomes deeper and slower. Continue to lengthen your breathing. With each breath in, the air is gathering any tension you have in your body. With each breath out, the stress and tension flow out through your arms and legs. All of the muscles in your body are feeling warm and relaxed.

Now go back through your memory stores, as if your life were pictures in a photo album. Continue looking at your memory pictures until you come to a snapshot of a time in your life when you were feeling calm, content, safe, warm, and happy. This may be a time when you were alone somewhere, or it may be a time when you were with people or a person you love. The snapshot may be from a vacation or it may be from a regular day in your life. The snapshot just needs to be one moment long.

If you have trouble getting a picture, you may need to go back even further in time, to when you were a young child. If you are still unable to find one, you can create one of your own by imagining yourself in the place you most want to be in the world.

Now take your snapshot and imagine yourself there in that moment, right now. What is going on around you? Who is with you? What do you see? What are your feelings in that moment? Feel the happiness of being in that moment. Feel the warmth of love around you. Feel the safety and security that comes from being in that special place. Feel the comfort of being relaxed and free of any worries. Let the feelings flow through you. What sounds do you hear? If you are outdoors, you may hear birds singing, the trees rustling in the wind, or waves rolling into shore. If you are indoors, you may hear a cat purring, laughter, or the sound of raindrops on the roof. What smells are around you? What does the air smell like? Let the warmth of the love around you wash over you. What do your surroundings feel like? If there is sunshine, feel the warmth of the sun on your face. If there is a fireplace, feel the warmth of the fire on your hands. Take all the time that you need to stay in your moment. As you stay in your moment, the stress and tension you were feeling is flowing out of your body and is replaced by the warmth, comfort, and safety of your image.

As you focus on your image, continue to breathe, slowly and regularly. With each breath in, the cleansing air is calming your spirits. With each breath out, your stress and tension are released. Breathe in slowly, one, two, three. Breathe out slowly, one, two, three. And in—one, two, three. And out—one, two, three. As you continue to breathe, your breathing becomes deeper and slower. Continue to lengthen your breathing. With each breath in the air is gathering any tension you have in your body. With each breath out, the stress and tension flow out through your arms and legs. All of the muscles in your body are feeling warm and relaxed. Continue to be in your moment. Remember what your body feels like to be in this moment. Whenever you need to come back, this moment will be here for you to bring you comfort and calm. Take all of the time that you need to be in this moment. When you are feeling ready, you can gradually come back to the room you are in and open your eyes. When you come back to the here and now, the good feelings and relaxation will stay with you throughout the day.

Doing this exercise regularly can help you develop skills to soothe and comfort yourself whenever you need to. You will be able to access self-soothing feelings by remembering how you felt during the exercise. We recommend that you practice this exercise at least once a day. Don't worry if you find other thoughts popping into your head as you are practicing the exercise. That is normal. Just let the thoughts go through your mind like cars on a country road. As the thought passes by, just direct your attention back to the exercise. Similarly, if you feel anxious as you practice the exercise, let any anxiety go and focus your attention back to the exercise.

Coping with Emotions

Another strategy for dealing with urges to self-harm is to manage your emotions more directly. The exercises and suggestions in chapter 8, where we discuss about identifying and coping with emotions, can help you here.

Connecting with Others

It is almost impossible to self-harm when you are around other people. When you are feeling urges to self-harm, a good strategy is to connect with other people. Call a family member, make plans with a friend, or get out to a public place. This will help you to ride out your urges and lessen your chances of acting on them.

Shifting Thoughts

Again, you can change how you feel by shifting your thoughts. Consider the following examples.

Self-Harm Thoughts	Realistic View
Hurting myself is the only way to feel better.	Hurting myself is one way to feel better, but there are other options as well. I can try the strategies I have learned. They may not work as fast or as effectively, but they are more healthy for me in the long run.
These horrible feelings will never go away.	Although it feels like these feelings are so powerful they will last forever, realistically I know they will pass. I have felt this way before and made it through. I can make it through this time.
These awful feelings are too overwhelming to cope with.	Just because I am feeling overwhelmed, doesn't mean I am overwhelmed. I can handle this situation by trying some more healthy coping strategies.
I am disgusting and deserve to be punished.	Just because I feel disgusting doesn't mean that I am. I have had bad things happen to me that have made me feel this way. I would never tell a friend that she should be punished because she feels bad about herself. I don't deserve to be punished either.
This numbness makes me feel dead.	I am feeling numb because I haven't been eating, and I have been dealing with some painful experiences that happened to me. There is a reason that I feel this way and I can take healthier steps to feel better, like normalizing my eating and working on my emotions.

Environmental Control

Take steps to keep your environment a safe one. If you use an object to hurt yourself, then you want to make sure that it is inaccessible or in the garbage. For example, Karen uses a utility knife to cut herself, so she makes sure she doesn't keep one in the house.

Use the Dealing with Self-Harm Worksheet to track your urges, to monitor triggers (situations, emotions), and to learn from your experiences.

Dealing with Urges to Self-Harm Worksheet

When you have an urge to self-harm, complete this worksheet. Record the situation or events leading up to the urge. Record how you are feeling and the intensity of each emotion from 0 (not at all) to 100 (most extreme). What thoughts are going through your mind? What strategies will you use to deal with your urge? Then record the outcome of the urge (Did you act on it? Did you sit through it? How long did it take to pass? How are you feeling now?).

Situation	Emotion(s)	Thoughts	Strategies	Outcome

Impulsive Behaviors

Bulimia has been associated with an increased risk of reckless or impulsive behaviors, involving a lack of consideration of the risks and consequences before taking action (Bell and Newns 2002). Impulsive behaviors include self-harm behaviors (covered above), alcohol and drug abuse, engaging in risky sexual encounters, compulsive shopping, and shoplifting (Lacey and Evans 1986). These behaviors are often associated with a feeling of being out of control, and attempts to suppress these behaviors often lead to intense negative emotion and discomfort.

The triggers for impulsive behaviors are different for each person and may be similar to the common triggers described above for self-harm behaviors including perception of a relationship loss, feelings of abandonment and isolation, overwhelming emotions such as extreme tension, anxiety, anger, and fear, feeling detached from yourself or what is going on around you, feeling numb or "nothing," or a need to express emotions or conflict.

The first step in dealing with your impulsive behaviors is to carefully analyze them. Use the following worksheet as a guide.

Functional Analysis Worksheet

1. Think back over your recent instances of impulsive behavior (alcohol and drug abuse, overdoses, risky sexual encounters, compulsive shopping or shoplifting). What were the *triggers* (the emotions, thoughts, or situations) that activated your urge for the impulsive behavior?

_____

_____

_____

2. Record your impulsive *behavior* by breaking it down into separate steps (for example, for shoplifting: left house, drove to mall, went into store, walked around until I found something I wanted, looked to see that no one was watching, put item under my coat, walked out).

Step 1. _____   Step 6. _____

Step 2. _____   Step 7. _____

Step 3. _____   Step 8. _____

Step 4. _____   Step 9. _____

Step 5. _____   Step 10. _____

3. What are the emotional and physical *consequences* of the behavior? Consequences may involve both benefits and costs. There are immediate consequences (get a

thrill, feel better, escape painful emotions), potential consequences (may get caught, could ruin my life), and long-term consequences (feel badly, feel out of control, worry about how this behavior could affect my job and relationships, shame) that you should identify. Look at the consequences in terms of these categories.

Immediate consequences: _____

_____

_____

_____

Potential consequences: _____

_____

_____

_____

Long-term consequences: _____

_____

_____

_____

4. How does engaging in the behavior fit with your values and goals for the future?

_____

_____

_____

Often a behavior can feel so automatic, you don't feel like you have any control to stop it. Once it starts, you feel like you have to complete the action. However, as we discussed, you can act otherwise. Earlier, you recorded your impulsive behavior as a series of steps. At each step, you can choose to stop and shift your direction. When you look at your behavior in this way, you can see many points where you can stop and take control. For each of the steps that you identified, record what you could have done at that moment to break the chain of events. There are likely a number of options. Write down as many options as you can think of for each step.

Steps	Other Options
1.	
2.	
3.	
4.	
5.	
6.	
7.	
8.	

Other Coping Strategies

Many of the coping strategies you've learned to avoid acting on eating disorder symptoms can help you with impulsive behaviors (see chapter 5). You can also use the same strategies that you would use to avoid self-harm, which we just covered. If you did not read that section, take some time now to review these strategies. Consider which ones you could use to manage your urge to engage in an impulsive behavior (problem solving, self-soothing, coping with emotions, shifting thoughts, connecting with others, or environmental control).

Substance Use

Studies show that up to 50 percent of individuals with bulimia also have a problem with substance use (Lilenfeld et al. 1997). Substances that are often associated with bulimia include alcohol, stimulants (diet pills or appetite suppressants), laxatives, diuretics and illegal or recreational drugs (Mitchell, Pomeroy, and Huber 1988). In this section, we will help you to identify whether substance use is a problem for you. We will also offer some strategies to help address substance use. Self-help strategies can address relatively mild problems with alcohol or drug use, but more serious problems involving alcohol and drug abuse or dependence are likely to require specialized help. If you think that you need help, see your family doctor for a referral to the appropriate service or agency.

Is Alcohol a Problem for You?

Drinking alcohol is socially acceptable in our society. Most celebrations or special occasions involve toasts with alcohol, and it is common to have wine with dinner or an after-dinner drink. So if it is okay to drink alcohol, how do you know if you have a problem? Complete the Drinking Behaviors Checklist, based on the criteria for alcohol abuse and dependence outlined in the *DSM-IV-TR* (APA 2000).

Drinking Behaviors Checklist

Answer each question below by placing an X in the Yes or No column.

		Yes	No
1.	Does your alcohol use interfere with your ability to perform what is expected of you at work, school, or home (missing work or school on multiple occasions, neglecting household tasks)?		
2.	Do you use alcohol in situations where it is physically dangerous (drinking and driving, drinking and operating a machine)?		
3.	Has your use of alcohol caused legal problems for you (being arrested for being intoxicated)?		
4.	Does your drinking interfere with your ability to normalize your eating (skipping meals and drinking instead)?		
5.	Has your use of alcohol affected your relationships (causing arguments with family members, strain on relationships)?		
6.	Do you find that you need to regularly increase the amount of alcohol you drink to achieve the same buzz or level of intoxication?		
7.	Do you notice that you don't get the same buzz or level of intoxication as you used to from the amount that you drink?		
8.	If you decrease the amount you drink, do you experience withdrawal symptoms (sweating, racing heart, shakiness, insomnia, nausea, restlessness, anxiety)?		
9.	Do you often drink more than you planned to?		
10.	Do you often drink for a longer period than you planned to?		
11.	Have you tried on a number of occasions to control or cut down on you drinking?		
12.	Have you unsuccessfully tried to quit drinking?		
13.	Do you find you spend a lot of time drinking or being hung over?		
14.	Have you reduced important social or recreational activities that you used to do because of your drinking?		
15.	Has your alcohol use caused or exacerbated physical or emotional problems?		
16.	Do you ever engage in binge drinking (drinking five or more drinks in one period of time)?		
17.	Does your drinking often lead to eating disorder symptoms (restricting, bingeing and vomiting)?		

If you answered any of the questions on the Drinking Behavior Checklist with a "yes," then it is likely that alcohol is a problem for you. You can use the strategies we have suggested in this chapter to try to make a change in your alcohol use. If this is too difficult, or you are unable to cut down on your own, it may be a sign that you need additional help.

Are Illegal or Recreational Drugs a Problem for You?

Research shows that bulimia is often associated with drug-use problems (amphetamines, barbiturates, marijuana, tranquilizers, ecstasy, and cocaine) (Wiederman and Pryor 1996). Appetite suppression may be one motivating factor for use of illegal drugs (Jonas et al. 1987). For example, Cindy reported that her main motivation for using cocaine was that it helped her to control her weight. In the next section, we will cover the different functions that your drug use may serve in your life. First, complete the Drug Use Behaviors Checklist, based on the criteria for substance abuse and dependence outlined in the *DSM-IV-TR* (APA 2000).

Drug Use Behaviors Checklist

Answer each question below by placing an X in the Yes or No column.

		Yes	No
1.	Does your drug use interfere with your ability to perform what is expected of you at work, school, or home (missing work or school on multiple occasions, neglecting household tasks)?		
2.	Do you use drugs in situations where it is physically dangerous (driving, operating machinery)?		
3.	Has your use of drugs caused legal problems for you (being arrested for behaviors performed when you were under the influence of drugs)?		
4.	Does your drug use interfere with your ability to normalize your eating (e.g., skipping meals and using drugs instead)?		
5.	Has your use of drugs affected your relationships (causing arguments with family members, strain on relationships)?		
6.	Do you find that you need to regularly increase the amount of drugs that you use to achieve the same buzz or high?		
7.	Do you notice that you don't get the same buzz or high as you used to from the amount of drugs that you use?		
8.	If you decrease the amount of drugs that you use, do you experience withdrawal symptoms (sweating, racing heart, shakiness, insomnia, nausea, restlessness, anxiety)?		

9.	Do you often use more of the drug than you planned to?		
10.	Do you often use the drug for a longer period than you planned to?		
11.	Have you tried on a number of occasions to control or cut down your use of drugs?		
12.	Have you unsuccessfully tried to quit drugs completely?		
13.	Do you find you spend a lot of time using drugs or recovering from the effects of using drugs?		
14.	Have you reduced important social or recreational activities that you used to do because of your drug use?		
15.	Has your drug use caused or exacerbated physical or emotional problems?		
16.	Does your drug use often lead to eating disorder symptoms (restricting, bingeing and vomiting)?		

If you answered any of the questions on this checklist with a "yes," then it is likely that drug use is a problem for you

Bulimia and Your Substance Use

Just as an eating disorder may be viewed as an unhealthy coping strategy, substance use may also occur as a way of coping. Individuals may use substances for a variety of reasons including:

* to avoid eating

* to control weight

* to suppress appetite

* to manage distress

* to escape negative feelings

* to escape problems

* to feel better.

What substance(s) are you using?

_____

_____

_____

How much and how often do you use this substance(s)?

_____

_____

_____

What does your substance use help you cope with?

_____

_____

_____

What costs and benefits do you experience as a result of your substance use? Consider time, cost, impact on relationships, impact on goals, impact on functioning at work or school, consequences to health, and effects on emotional well-being.

Benefits	Costs

How do the costs compare to the benefits of your substance use?

_____

_____

_____

_____

Where Do You Start?

Recovery from bulimia is about becoming healthy and identifying the issues that are driving your eating disorder. Substance use runs contrary to recovery by fueling the eating disorder and masking the important issues that you are trying to tackle. If you are not able to quit completely, you can try tapering your substance use over time. Use the Monitoring Substance Use Worksheet to help you stay on top of your progress. It is a good idea to make some copies of the worksheet so you can monitor your use over time. Alternatively, you can re-create the monitoring sheet in a journal.

Monitoring Substance Use Worksheet

Set a target goal for the week of what your limit will be for the substance. On the graph below, monitor the amount you use the substance on a daily basis by filling in the number of boxes that correspond to how much you used the substance for that day. At the end of the week, check to see how your actual use compares to your goal. This graph is set to monitor an amount ranging from 0 to 20. If your use is more than 20 (20 drinks, 20 pills), you can renumber the lefthand side of the graph or create your own graph.

Goal: _____

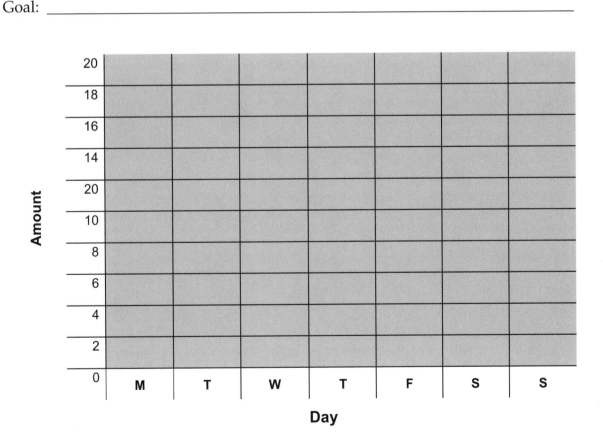

Dealing with Substance-Related Urges

You can apply all of the skills that you have learned as you worked through this book to deal with your urges for substance use. Consider which of the strategies you could use to manage your urge for substance use (problem solving, self-soothing, coping with emotions, shifting thoughts, connecting with others, or environmental control). Remember, you have to keep an open mind and try each strategy before you can determine whether it is helpful or not.

Chapter 10

Managing Depression and Anxiety

The purpose of this chapter is to help you to identify problems with depression and anxiety that you may be struggling with and to provide you with strategies to manage associated symptoms. Many of the strategies will build upon the work that you have already done. This chapter is a good starting point for tackling these problems, however, if you feel that you are not able to control your feelings of depression and anxiety, or if your mood and anxiety symptoms are causing you significant distress, you should seek additional help.

If you are having no difficulties with a problem covered in this chapter, just skip the section in question. Or, if you are experiencing no difficulty with any of the problems covered in this chapter, move on to chapter 11.

Depression

When you are struggling with bulimia, it is very likely that you are experiencing symptoms of depression as well. When you are depressed, you feel sad and down for most of the day, nearly every day for at least two weeks or more. You may also find that you are not interested in the things you used to enjoy, or that you no longer experience pleasure from doing the things you used to love. For example, you may no longer feel like going out with friends or you may no longer enjoy watching a movie or reading a book. Depressed mood and lack of enjoyment may also be accompanied by other symptoms of depression, including:

* change in your appetite (eating more or less than is usual for you)

* disturbed sleeping patterns (sleeping more or less than usual, difficulty falling asleep, or difficulty staying asleep)

* feeling physically restless or sluggishly slow

* loss of energy

* feelings of worthlessness

* difficulty thinking or concentrating

* thoughts of death or suicide (APA 2000).

Many of these symptoms may actually be a consequence of your bulimia (appetite changes, difficulties sleeping, feelings of worthlessness, difficulty concentrating, and lack of energy). That is why it is hard to treat depression when someone is actively engaging in eating disorder behaviors. Research studies indicate high rates of depression in individuals with bulimia nervosa, with estimates ranging from 30 to 70 percent (Lee, Rush, and Mitchell 1985). Individuals with depression and bulimia have higher levels of body dissatisfaction than do individuals with bulimia only (Bulik et al. 1996). Symptoms of depression may be a contributing factor to increased body dissatisfaction (Keel et al. 2001).

Your feelings of depression may have started before your bulimia, or your depression may have come later, after the eating disorder took hold. We know from research that in most cases depression comes after the bulimia, a consequence of chaotic eating, purging, and preoccupation with weight and shape (Steere, Butler, and Cooper 1990). The best course of action is to normalize your eating and eliminate your eating disorder behaviors to see what effect this has on your mood. Your depressive symptoms may disappear. If your depression persists, it may require special attention on its own.

Taking Control of Your Mood

When you are feeling depressed, you are no longer active in the things that gave you pleasure. You are not only feeling down; you are also not experiencing the things that make you feel good. This withdrawal from life activities helps to maintain feelings of depression.

Behavioral Activation

Behavioral activation is a set of strategies that combats depression by focusing on decreasing withdrawal and inactivity and reconnecting with activities associated with pleasure and enjoyment. Try the following behavioral activation strategies based on the work of Jacobson, Martell, and Dimidjian (2001) to help improve your mood.

Develop a regular routine. When you are depressed, you may not feel like getting out of bed, let alone having a shower, doing your hair or makeup, and making sure you are dressed nicely. You may also not care about following a normalized eating plan. This lack of structure allows lots of time for you to feel worse about yourself. The first step in feeling better is to set up a structure for a daily routine. This means planning out the times when you will wake up, go to work or school, go to bed, and eat your meals.

If you continue to wait until you feel like doing something, you may wait forever. In reality, relief from depressive feelings often comes *after* changing your behavior and not before. Once you get into a basic routine of getting up, getting ready for the day, having breakfast, and so on, you will start to notice that your mood improves as well. Consider the following case.

Lisa had been feeling so depressed, she found that she would sleep in until noon. When she woke up, she would have very little energy and would stay in her pajamas throughout the day, unless she absolutely had to go out. When she did have to go out, just having a shower was an enormous task, because she wasn't used to it. At night, she would have difficulty falling asleep, so she would stay up very late watching television until she would fall asleep on the couch. She rarely ate throughout the day and found herself bingeing late at night. She no longer did the things she used to enjoy, like taking her dogs for walks, reading, or painting. Lisa was between jobs and found that she had no motivation to even think of looking for a job or even update her resume. She felt bad about herself, and she felt even worse because she didn't do anything in the day except sit on the couch.

The first step for Lisa was to establish a daily routine. She used an activity log to schedule her daily routine and activities. She found that this helped give her structure and momentum throughout the day. She didn't have to think about what she would do, she just looked at the activity log and tried to follow it. Lisa also scheduled in times to do things that she previously enjoyed (calling a friend, walking the dog, and painting). Lisa scheduled 9 A.M. as her wake up time and midnight as her bedtime. After just a week of following the schedule, Lisa noticed her mood was slightly improved and that she had more energy. After another week, she found that her sleeping wasn't as disturbed and she was starting to enjoy activities that she hadn't for a long time. Lisa really found the activity log helpful for keeping her routine and sticking to it. Even if she had no outside activities planned, she started each day having a shower and getting ready, as if she were going out. She found that over time her mood continued to improve and her depressive symptoms decreased.

You can try using an activity log and see how it works for you. Complete the Activity Log Worksheet by scheduling in the following things hour by hour:

* when you will wake up and go to bed

* when you will eat throughout the day (aiming for three meals a day)

* what activities you will do in the morning, afternoon, and evening

* one fun activity *every* day (you may need to rely on what used to give you pleasure in the past to decide on what you will schedule).

Activity Log Worksheet

Schedule your activities for the week including your basic daily routine (wake up time, bed time, meal times, and activities). Plan at least one activity every day that is for pleasure.

	Monday	Tuesday	Wednesday	Thursday	Friday	Saturday	Sunday
8:00							
9:00							
10:00							
11:00							
Noon							
1:00							
2:00							
3:00							
4:00							
5:00							
6:00							
7:00							
8:00							
9:00							
10:00							
11:00							
Mid-night							

Notice your mood changes. After you have followed your activity log for one week, start to notice how changes in your mood correspond with changes in your behavior. If you mood is down during certain times of the day, what are you doing? What is going on in your life? For example, Lisa had scheduled having a bath as a fun activity. However, she noticed that whenever she had a bath, her mood was worse. When she examined the situation, she realized that when she was in the bath, she would ruminate about all of the things that she wasn't doing. No wonder she felt worse! There are two options for dealing with this situation. One is to try a different activity that is more mentally engaging. The second option is to mentally engage in the activity you are doing, so that you are fully experiencing it. For Lisa, this meant consciously letting her worries go when she would get into the bath. She would remind herself that this was her time to relax. She would listen to music and pay attention to the experience. In other words, she was practicing mindfulness during her bath. For Lisa, engaging in the activity and staying in the moment made a big difference. She was now able to really enjoy her bath without using the time to focus on depressive thoughts.

When you notice that your mood is down at a certain time of the day, check things out to see what you are doing and what you are thinking. Use this information to counteract your depression by actively experiencing what is going on around you instead of living in your head or in the past.

Decrease avoidance and withdrawal. As you continue to follow the activity log, work on identifying situations that you have been avoiding because you didn't feel up to them. Start to incorporate avoided activities each week. If you have been avoiding social activities, try scheduling in a social activity once a week (calling a friend, meeting a friend for coffee, going to your local community center, volunteering). You will likely be surprised by the outcome.

Challenging Negative Thoughts

The techniques you learned in chapter 6 to shift your eating disorder thoughts were originally pioneered for treatment of depression (Beck et al. 1979). The cognitive strategies suggested in this chapter are based on this same material, as well as the work of David Burns (1999). According to the cognitive approach, the way you feel is a consequence of the way that you interpret, perceive, or make sense of what is going on around you (Beck 1964). If your perceptions, thoughts, and beliefs are negative, then you will feel depressed. By changing how you think, you can change how you feel.

If you are depressed, it can be helpful to look at thought distortions which may be making you feel down. We have already covered some thought distortions, and we list them below, along with some cognitive distortions that are commonly linked to depression. Do these distortions sound familiar?

❋ **Emotional reasoning:** You feel something is true. Therefore it is. Example: You feel like a loser; therefore you are a loser. Or you feel out of control; therefore you are out of control.

❋ **Scale self-esteem:** The number on the scale determines your worth as a person. Example: You are unhappy with your weight and feel like you are not good enough as a person.

❋ **Social comparison:** You compare yourself to others, and you always lose. Others are always thinner, more attractive, more successful, more intelligent, and more put together. Example: You go to a party and feel bad about yourself because everyone looks thinner and more attractive than you.

❋ **Feeling fat:** You feel sad, hopeless, dejected, disgusting, pathetic, ugly, worthless, incompetent, humiliated, lonely, overwhelmed, scared, and any other negative adjective that would apply. Example: You are out at dinner with another couple and feel that you are not as successful as everyone else. You increasingly "feel fat" and don't feel like you should be eating. Deep down you feel inadequate.

❋ **Thinking in extremes:** You see things as black or white, all or nothing. Example: When you follow your eating rules you feel good about yourself but when you "slip up" you feel horrible and pathetic.

❋ **Changing how you feel by changing your size:** You think that by changing your weight, you can magically change other aspects of your life that are unrelated to weight. Example: You feel that if you lost a few pounds, you would feel better about yourself and everything would fall into place with other things in your life.

❋ **Harsh self-judgment:** Labeling and criticizing yourself in a negative manner in a way that you would never do to anyone else. Example: You think of yourself as "pathetic" and a "loser" because you are unsure about your future. Or you think of yourself as a "pig" and "disgusting" because you ate dessert.

❋ **Jumping to conclusions:** You make assumptions about what people think or about the future that are based on how you feel and not on the facts. Example: You feel like your future is hopeless and things will never get better. Or you assume that people are negatively evaluating you similar to the way you negatively evaluate yourself.

❋ **Focusing on the negative:** You focus on the negative aspects of yourself, others, and your future and ignore neutral or positive aspects. Example: You feel that your future is hopeless and focus on what you don't have while ignoring all of the opportunities that you do have. You feel like a failure as a person, but you are ignoring all of the wonderful things that you have done for others and your family.

After reviewing the following example, you can use a Thought Monitoring Worksheet to work with negative thoughts that fuel your feelings of depression. Note: In addition to eating disorder symptoms, you may have urges to self-harm, or engage in reckless behaviors or substance abuse (covered in chapter 9). If so, note the feelings you have that accompany these urges, along with the feelings that accompany eating disorder symptoms.

Thought Monitoring Example			
Feeling(s) and Urges Rate (0–100)	**Situation/Trigger**	**Thoughts**	**Distortions**
depressed (90) *hopeless (80)*	*Went to a party where everyone seemed successful and confident except me.*	*I don't know what I am doing with my life. Things aren't going to get better. Everyone else is better than me. I am pathetic.*	*thinking in extremes* *jumping to conclusions* *social comparison* *harsh self-judgment/ emotional reasoning*
depressed (90) *overwhelmed (85)* *sad (80)* *hopeless (95)*	*No trigger that I can think of. Woke up feeling horrible and depressed.*	*I will always feel this way. I will never feel better. I can't manage these feelings. I can't go on feeling horrible like this. My life is terrible.*	*jumping to conclusions* *thinking in extremes* *emotional reasoning* *focusing on the negative*
lonely (90) *inadequate (70)* *sad (80)* *hopeless (60)*	*Found out ex is in a new relationship.*	*His new partner is probably more attractive and successful than I am. I will never find someone else. I will be alone forever.*	*social comparison* *jumping to conclusions* *emotional reasoning* *harsh self-judgment* *thinking in extremes* *focusing on the negative*

Thought Monitoring Worksheet

Over the next week, use this sheet to monitor your thoughts whenever you notice a downward shift in how you are feeling or when you have urges for eating disorder symptoms, self-harm, reckless behaviors, or substance use. Record what feelings you are experiencing and the intensity of each feeling from 0 (not at all) to 100 (most extreme). Record the situation or trigger associated with the feeling(s). Record any thoughts that were going through your mind at the time. Examine the thoughts you had for any distortions and record them. Identify as many distortions as you can for each thought.

Feeling(s) and Urges Rate (0–100)	Situation/Trigger	Thoughts	Distortions

Thought Monitoring Review

After you have monitored your thoughts for a week, examine your Thought Monitoring Worksheet. Look for connections between your feelings and thoughts and the situations or triggers. What do you notice?

_____

_____

_____

_____

Do you see any patterns in these connections?

_____

_____

_____

_____

Are there common triggers or situations?

_____

_____

_____

_____

Do you see any recurring thought distortions?

_____

_____

_____

_____

If you have difficulty answering these questions or if you have had difficulty identifying your thoughts or thought distortions, continue monitoring for another week. As you become more aware of the connection between situations or triggers and your thoughts and feelings, it will become easier to identify problematic thoughts and thought distortions that fuel your depression.

Shifting Your Negative Thoughts

Once you have practiced identifying thought distortions related to your feelings of depression, you are ready to practice shifting your negative thoughts following the same process you learned in chapter 6. Remember, the goal is to widen your perspective so that you can come up with a more balanced or realistic view. As you practice taking on a more balanced view, you will notice that your depression is reduced and you are feeling better. Again, the technique of shifting your thinking doesn't lead to results overnight, but with practice, over time it will become easier to shift your negative thoughts and you will find that you are no longer reacting to triggers in the same way. You will also notice that you have more control over how you *choose* to react to a situation.

Practice counteracting your negative thoughts using the Shifting Negative Thoughts Worksheet. Make copies, so you can complete the worksheet whenever you notice a fluctuation in your mood or urges for eating disorder symptoms, self-harm, reckless behaviors, or substance use. We've included a couple of examples for you to review.

Note: If you have trouble generating alternative ways of thinking about the situation (the "realistic view"), ask yourself the following questions:

* How would someone without an eating disorder think about this situation?

* What would someone who was not depressed say about this situation?

* What advice would a friend give me if he or she knew I felt this way?

* Am I ignoring positive aspects about myself?

* What would I say to a friend who felt this way?

* How helpful is this way of thinking?

* What impact does this way of thinking have on my life?

Shifting Negative Thoughts Example

Feeling(s) and Urges Rate (0–100)	Situation or Trigger	Problematic Thoughts	Realistic View	Rerate Feelings (0–100)	Outcome
depressed (90) *hopeless (80)*	*Went to a party where everyone seemed successful and confident except me.*	*I don't know what I am doing with my life. Things aren't going to get better. Everyone else is better than me. I am pathetic.*	*It is not really true that I don't know what I am doing with my life. I have some ideas. It is just taking me a while to sort out what path I want to take. I am "thinking in extremes"—just because I don't have everything figured out doesn't mean that I have nothing figured out. When I compare myself to others, it's not helpful. It doesn't matter what other people are doing. I just need to focus on me. Also, just because it seems like everyone is successful doesn't mean it is true. I don't really know what difficulties these people may be facing. And what is "pathetic," anyway? I have lots of positive qualities that I am ignoring. I would never call one of my friends pathetic, so I will not do that to myself, either. There are probably other people here that feel like they do not measure up, as well. The real issue for me is feeling better about myself and I have already started to work on this by writing all this down!*	*depressed (50)* *hopeless (40)*	*I was able to stop focusing on other people and actually focus on the conversation. Although some people were obnoxious, I met a few people who were very nice. I had a better time than I thought I would.*

Shifting Negative Thoughts Example

Feeling(s) and Urges Rate (0–100)	Situation or Trigger	Problematic Thoughts	Realistic View	Rerate Feelings (0–100)	Outcome
depressed (90) *over-whelmed (85)* *sad (80)* *hopeless (95)*	*No trigger that I can think of. Woke up feeling horrible and depressed.*	*I will always feel this way. I will never feel better. I can't manage these feelings. I can't go on feeling horrible like this. My life is terrible.*	*It is not true that I will always feel this way. I have felt this way before, and the feelings do pass. I just have to ride them out. Just because I feel that I can't manage doesn't mean it is true (this is emotional reasoning). I will try to use some of the strategies I have learned in this book. I am focusing on the negative. My life isn't completely terrible. There are some good aspects that are hard for me to think about now. I just need to hang in there and keep going. These horrible feelings will pass. In fact, one positive is that I made it through these feelings before, which is evidence that I will make it through this time as well.*	*depressed (60)* *over-whelmed (65)* *sad (50)* *hopeless (30)*	*Called a friend and made a plan to go out, even though I didn't feel up to it. Found that part way through the day, I started to feel much better.*

Shifting Negative Thoughts Worksheet

Over the next week, use this sheet to monitor your thoughts and counteract negative thoughts whenever you notice a downward shift in how you are feeling or urges to have symptoms, engage in self-harm, reckless behaviors, or substance use. Record what feelings you are experiencing and the intensity of each feeling from 0 (not at all) to 100 (most extreme). Record the situation or trigger associated with the feeling(s). Record any thoughts that were going through your mind at the time. Examine the thoughts for any distortions. Counteract the distortions or negative thoughts. Rerate your feelings (0 to 100) and then record the outcome or how you responded to the situation or trigger.

Feeling(s) and Urges Rate (0–100)	Situation or Trigger	Problematic Thoughts	Realistic View (How would someone without an eating disorder think about this situation? What would someone who was not depressed say about this situation? What advice would a friend give me if he or she knew I felt this way? Am I ignoring positive aspects about myself? What are alternative ways of interpreting this situation? What would I say to a friend who felt this way? How helpful is this way of thinking?)	Rerate Feelings (0–100)	Outcome

Shifting Negative Thoughts Review

After you have practice counteracting your negative thoughts for a week, are there any counteracting thoughts that are particularly useful or powerful for you (for example, "I am an island," "Just because I feel it, doesn't mean it is true," "It is okay to have these feelings," "I am a worthwhile person.")?

_____

_____

_____

_____

_____

Did you notice your mood shift depending on what you were thinking?

_____

_____

_____

_____

Shifting Core Beliefs

As we have discussed, core beliefs are the deeply held beliefs that you hold about yourself, others, and the world around you, and the future. These absolute and rigid beliefs are the driving force behind your negative thoughts and contribute to depression. You can also use the Shifting Core Beliefs Worksheet (from chapter 8) to modify core beliefs that you become aware of, as you shift your negative thoughts. Remember, negative thoughts are specific to the situation or trigger, whereas core beliefs are more generalized statements about yourself, others, and your future.

Coping with Crisis

Again, if your depression is interfering with your life and causing you great distress, you should seek further help. Chapter 13 goes into different kinds of therapy that might benefit you. Some people who are dealing with depression may become so hopeless that they contemplate suicide. If you have ever felt suicidal, you should keep a card easily accessible where you have written down whom to call (a friend, family member, doctor, or emergency number) in the event that these thoughts or feelings return. Local crisis lines are usually listed in the front of the phone book. Suicidal thoughts or intentions are a symptom of distress; as with other symptoms, your job is to seek appropriate support and to make a plan for managing the symptom.

Anxiety

It is normal to experience anxiety and fear, and we have all had these feelings at some point in our lives. However, when anxiety occurs too frequently, is too intense, leads to considerable distress, or interferes in your life and your functioning, it has become a problem that is worthy of attention. When you have bulimia, you may also be struggling with an anxiety problem as well. Research indicates that anxiety disorders occur at a higher rate in individuals with bulimia nervosa than in individuals without bulimia nervosa (Godart et al. 2002). For example, one study found that 64 percent of women with bulimia nervosa also had an anxiety disorder, and in most cases, the anxiety disorder began much earlier than did the bulimia (Bulik et al. 1996). Another study found that in 53.9 percent of cases, the anxiety disorder preceded the onset of the bulimia (Schwalberg et al. 1992). Research indicates that some anxiety disorders have been found to be particularly associated with bulimia including social anxiety disorder, generalized anxiety disorder and obsessive compulsive disorder. Our strategies for handling anxiety are based on work by Barlow and Craske (1994), Beck, Greenberg, and Emery (1990), and Wells (1997).

Social Anxiety

Social anxiety involves fear of negative evaluation by others. It may be accompanied by nervousness or discomfort in social situations, or avoidance of social situations (APA 2000). Social anxiety may be separate from your eating disorder, or it may be related to your eating disorder in a few ways including social anxiety related to appearance, weight and shape, and eating. Research indicates that very often, individuals with bulimia are concerned not only with how others will view their physical presentation but also how others will perceive them in general (Striegel-Moore, Silberstein, and Rodin 1993). Studies indicate that social anxiety disorder is more common in individuals with bulimia than in individuals without bulimia (Godart et al. 2002).

For example, Morgan is a twenty-seven-year-old woman who works at an accounting firm. She described having always been shy. As she went through school she remembered being teased about the way that she looked. She worried a lot about how she came across to other people and the impression that she made on them. In high school, she began to avoid social activities like parties and dances because of fear that her peers would think she was stupid. She also avoided speaking in public, answering questions in class, and giving class presentations because of fear that she would make a mistake and look foolish. In college, Morgan became more concerned about how she looked and began to try to change her appearance through dieting. This led to a struggle with bulimia. Morgan went for treatment for her bulimia. During her recovery, it became clear that her anxiety in social situations was a significant problem for her and helped to fuel her eating disorder. Once Morgan had her bulimic symptoms under control, she began to work on managing her anxiety in social situations.

Strategies for Managing Social Anxiety

The strategies for managing social anxiety build on what you have learned throughout this book. The two main strategies are challenging anxious thoughts and confronting the situations you fear, adapted from Antony and Swinson (2000).

Challenging anxious thoughts. Just as you have learned to shift your eating disorder thoughts and negative thoughts, you can use the same technique for identifying and shifting anxious thoughts. The next time you are anxious, use the Shifting Anxious Thoughts Worksheet to record your anxious thoughts. Examine your anxious thoughts for distortions. Anxious distortions usually involve overestimating the likelihood of a bad event happening, exaggerating the negative consequences associated with an outcome, and underestimating your ability to cope. Once you have identified the distortions, you can then practice shifting your anxious thoughts by considering the realistic likelihood of the bad event happening, the realistic worst-case scenario, which is usually never as bad as you imagine, and your true ability to cope with the situation. It is also helpful to consider how you have managed in the past. Some helpful counteracting thoughts for social anxiety include:

* "So what if I look stupid. Big deal."

* "It is okay if someone doesn't like me. It's impossible to please everyone all of the time."

* "If someone does think negatively about me, that person is not worth my time."

* "It is okay to feel embarrassed. Embarrassment doesn't last forever. I certainly won't remember this situation when I am an eighty-year-old grandparent!"

* "People are generally thinking about themselves and not focusing on me."

Shifting Anxious Thoughts Worksheet

Over the next week, use this sheet to monitor your thoughts whenever you feel anxious. Record your level of anxiety from 0 (not at all) to 100 (most extreme). Record the situation or trigger associated with your anxiety. Record any thoughts that were going through your mind at the time. Examine the thoughts for any distortions (overestimation of the danger- ousness of the situation, exaggeration of the negative consequences, and under- estimation of your ability to cope). Rerate your anxiety (0 to 100) and then record the outcome or how you responded to the situation or trigger.

Anxiety Level Rate (0–100)	Situation or Trigger	Anxious Thoughts	Realistic View (What is the realistic likelihood that my feared prediction will come true? What happened when I was in this situation in the past? What is really the worst thing that could happen in this situation? What advice would a friend give me if he or she knew I felt this way? Am I ignoring positive aspects about myself? What are alternative ways of interpreting this situation? What would I say to a friend who felt this way?)	Rerate Anxiety (0–100)	Outcome

Confronting the situations that you fear. The second strategy for managing social anxiety is to gradually start to confront the situations that you fear. This means gradually eliminating avoidance from your life (for example, of certain social situations, or of being assertive). There are a number of reasons for facing what you fear:

* You will learn that your anxiety decreases.

* You get opportunities to practice challenging your anxious thoughts.

* You see that the negative consequences aren't as bad as you thought.

* You learn that you are able to manage better than you predicted.

* You gain confidence that you are tackling your fear.

* You develop your skills in social situations.

Generalized Anxiety

Generalized anxiety involves excessive and uncontrollable worries about a number of different areas that may include work or school performance, minor matters, physical health and safety, activities of family members, and appearance. If you have generalized anxiety, you may also feel restless, tired or irritable, or have headaches or muscle tension or difficulty concentrating or sleeping (APA 2000). Studies indicate that individuals with bulimia have a higher risk of developing generalized anxiety disorder at some point in their life than do individuals without bulimia (Godart et al. 2002). Strategies for managing your excessive worries include relaxation, shifting your anxious thoughts, not going there, problem solving, and remembering that just because you feel that way doesn't mean it's true.

* **Relaxation.** Use the techniques covered in this book to develop your ability to relax. Practicing relaxation strategies will help to decrease your stress and muscle tension and you will notice that you feel calmer and less agitated. You can use the guided imagery exercise from chapter 9. You can also use the mindfulness techniques described in chapter 5. Remember, it may take practice for you to achieve a state of relaxation.

* **Shifting your anxious thoughts.** Use the Shifting Anxious Thoughts Worksheet to challenge your worries.

* **Not going there.** Often when your worries are triggered, you have a choice. You can go down the worry path and think of all of the "what ifs," or you can move on. Being aware of this choice is useful. You can say to yourself, "Don't even go there!" and choose not go down the worry path.

- ❋ **Problem solving.** Instead of worrying about the "what ifs," you can use the Problem-Solving Technique covered in chapter 9 to tackle your problems head on.

- ❋ **Remember that just because you feel it doesn't mean it's true!** Often people have a worry and treat the worry as if it were almost a fact. It can be very powerful to remind yourself that your fear is just a worry thought, and even though you feel something bad is likely to happen doesn't mean that it will happen. You may want to write down the above phrase on a card that you can use to remind yourself whenever you find your worries gearing up.

Obsessive Compulsive Disorder

Obsessive compulsive disorder involves obsessions (recurrent intrusive thoughts, images, or impulses that are highly disturbing, such as thoughts about contamination, doubting whether you performed a behavior, and aggressive urges) and/or compulsions (repetitive rituals that are time-consuming and often serve to reduce the anxiety or discomfort triggered by the obsession, such as repeatedly washing, cleaning, or checking) (APA 2000). For some people, the obsessions and compulsions are closely connected to their eating disorder and involve obsessions about weight gain (such as thoughts that you have gained weight from touching something) and compulsions around eating disorder symptoms (vomiting, bingeing, exercise), food choices, and eating. Obsessive compulsive disorder tends to occur more frequently in individuals with bulimia than in individuals without bulimia (Lilienfeld et al. 1998). Strategies for managing obsessions and compulsions include changing your response to the obsession, riding out the obsession, eliminating the compulsion, and eliminating avoidance.

Changing your response to the obsession. An obsession is just a thought, although it often feels as if it is much more than that. If you start to treat the obsession as just a nuisance thought, it will start to lose its power. You can use the strategy from above, "Just because I think it, doesn't mean it's true!"

Riding out the obsession. When an obsession is triggered, if you ride it out without responding to it (with a certain behavior or compulsion), you will find that it loses its power over time and your anxiety will decrease. It is like an urge for an eating disorder symptom. It may help to review the strategies for managing urges that we covered in chapter 5.

Eliminating the compulsion. Compulsions serve to maintain the power of the obsession. When you do a compulsion, it reduces your anxiety so that the next time you feel anxious you have an even stronger urge to perform the compulsion.

If you cannot eliminate a compulsion completely at first, you can try to decrease it. For example, instead of checking something five times, you can try to check just once. If your compulsion is to eat things a certain way, you can try to change your routine, which will take some of the power out of the ritual. For example, if you usually eat breakfast timing each bite and chewing a certain number of times, you can try to eat your breakfast in a shorter time period, without counting each time you chew.

Eliminating avoidance. As with other anxiety problems, avoidance just serves to maintain anxiety. You may find that you are avoiding cues that trigger your obsessions and compulsions. Try to gradually confront the situations that you are avoiding so that you can practice the strategies that you have learned to manage your obsessions and compulsions and learn over time not to fear these situations.

Other Anxiety Problems

It is beyond the scope of this book to cover anxiety problems comprehensively. If you are dealing with anxiety and it's overwhelming for you, it is a good idea to consult your family doctor to learn about treatment options. There are also many good self-help books on specific anxiety disorders. Regardless of the nature of your anxiety problem, remember that anxiety is not dangerous. Although it may feel that your anxiety will build until it reaches an uncontrollable level and something disastrous will happen, the worst thing that can happen when you are anxious is that you will feel very, very uncomfortable. Over time, your anxiety will decrease. The more you practice riding the wave of anxiety, the more confident you will become in your ability to manage those uncomfortable physical sensations.

Chapter 11

Family Issues and Support

One of the factors that can contribute to developing and maintaining bulimia is the way your family functions. In some cases, the impact is obvious such as when sexual or physical abuse, substance abuse, or neglect is present. In other cases, the factors are much more subtle, such as when there are expectations, inconsistent rules, or comments that reinforce a focus on appearance. We realize that this may be an area that is very difficult for you to explore, and it can be especially hard if you have a good relationship with your family. When you explore these concerns, you may feel like you don't appreciate or love your family, or that you are blaming them for your eating disorder. This can lead to feelings of guilt and anxiety. If you feel this way, remember that the point is not to blame or judge your family, but rather to understand family factors that may have contributed to your bulimia, and learn to cope with these issues differently. In this chapter, we will cover ways to understand and manage some of these factors, as well as methods of obtaining support from your family and friends as you continue your journey toward recovery.

Family Functions

Bulimia can play an important role in the family or in other personal relationships. It is important to figure out what this role is, so that you can change your approach in your family or your relationships to increase your chances at recovery. Consider the following cases.

Holding the Family Together

Victoria has struggled with anorexia and bulimia for the last few years. She lives at home with her mother and father and younger sister. She completed intensive treatment four times and always gained weight to a healthy weight, normalized her eating, and stopped bingeing and vomiting. However, when the treatment ended, Victoria was able to hold onto her progress for only a few months before she started to lose weight and become symptomatic again. Her mother and father's relationship had never been good, and they had been talking about a divorce for the last five years. At times, this included her father moving out of the house or going on extended business trips. Each time Victoria's mother and father got close to finalizing their arrangements to separate, Victoria's eating disorder took a turn for the worse. When this happened, the family responded by regrouping and coming to her aid. Her father would fly home early, move back into the family house, and have long discussions with her mother about how to handle the eating disorder. Usually, they would try to increase the amount of time they spent together as a family. Victoria learned, quite correctly, that her eating disorder was the only thing that was holding her family together. As long as this dynamic continued, it was unlikely that Victoria would be able to recover from her eating disorder. The family function of the eating disorder was too powerful. It wasn't until her mother and father went ahead with their separation and divorce that Victoria was able to finally recover.

Diverting Attention from Other Problems

Jody's mother and father were very worried about her and they spent a great deal of time trying to speak with her and to help her with her eating disorder. They attended a number of family therapy sessions with Jody, and a weekly support group for family members and friends. Jody's mother described constantly worrying about Jody to the extent that she would lie awake at night and listen for Jody's footsteps to the kitchen to binge. Jody's dad spent a lot of time reading about bulimia and trying to prepare foods that he thought Jody would eat and not vomit. Jody's bulimia consumed her family.

During a family therapy session the therapist asked the family what they would worry about if they didn't have Jody's eating disorder to think about. Jody's dad responded that he would worry about his wife's drinking. Although this was a shock for Jody's mother, she agreed that this was a serious problem that needed to be addressed. Up until this point, Jody's eating disorder was doing a good job of protecting her mother from facing an embarrassing and difficult situation.

Fostering Relationships

Lynda and Andrea were friends who met during group treatment for their bulimia. During their treatment they related to one another on a variety of different issues and they developed a fast friendship. They talked about their struggles with bulimia, how bulimia had impacted their life, how difficult recovery was, normalized eating, strategies, and body image concerns. They would often get together for meals in order to support each other during difficult times. As they continued with their recovery and their friendship, Lynda realized that she was not enjoying her time with Andrea as much as she had in the past. She was tired of talking about bulimia and wanted to pursue other interests and conversations. The next time she met with Andrea, she expressed her concerns and asked her if they could not spend all of their time talking about eating disorders. Andrea agreed and thought this was a good idea, but much to their dismay they soon realized that they did not share common interests or backgrounds other than their eating disorder. Lynda realized that her friendship with Andrea was preventing her from fully recovering from her bulimia. For Lynda to move on with her life, it meant losing her friendship with Andrea.

Think about your family dynamic and your relationships with individual family members and friends, and consider how your eating disorder may serve a function or a purpose within each relationship. It is probably clear to you how recovery from your bulimia might benefit the people in your life, such as decreasing stress and tension, and increasing time to pursue other activities and interactions. It is also helpful to imagine negative consequences that might happen to your family and your relationships if you no longer had bulimia. For example, let's say you woke up tomorrow and you were completely cured of bulimia. How would relationships change in your family? Would someone else be in the hot seat? Would family members grow apart? How would your interactions change? What would you talk about? Would your family member or friend experience a loss or feel threatened?

Think about your relationships. What relationships (immediate family, partner, best friend) would be affected if you were to recover from bulimia?

_____

_____

_____

How would the relationships you have identified be affected by your recovery?

_____

_____

_____

What role does your bulimia play in these relationships?

_____

_____

_____

Family Rules

Most families operate with rules. Some rules may be stated explicitly such as "clean up after yourself" or "be home by midnight." Although rules are necessary for a family to function, rules that are excessive, inappropriate, inconsistent, or unclear can leave you feeling ineffective or out of control. These feelings can contribute to low self-esteem, eating disorder symptoms, and other problems. Ideally, rules should have a rationale that makes sense, and be clear and consistent. Although consistency is important, rigidity can be problematic. Under ideal conditions, rules are negotiated over time and adapt to the changing needs of the family and each individual.

Other family rules are not necessarily spoken. For example, Heather grew up in a small town with her mother, father, and two older brothers. Her father had experienced a work-related accident ten years ago, and subsequently was on disability and suffering from chronic back pain. Since the accident, Heather's mother had tried to reduce all unpleasantness in the home, and the golden unspoken rule was "don't upset your father." Heather's brothers were not very good at following this rule and often would get into trouble at school and end up in loud arguments with their father.

Heather felt her role was to keep the peace at home. As a result, she never disobeyed her parents, always put on a happy face, despite how she was feeling, and only spoke of positive events and feelings. The family rule sent the message to Heather that her needs and emotions were not important or necessary, and that she was responsible for the happiness of the household and for providing relief to her father's pain. Heather ended up feeling anxious and guilty most of the time, and learned to suppress her needs and her emotions through bingeing and vomiting.

Other implicit or unspoken family rules may include:

* Don't discuss family issues outside of the family.

* Never argue or express your concerns.

* Don't talk back.

* Don't show your emotions in public.

* Emotions are weak or unnecessary.

* Don't complain.

* Be productive at all times.

✸ Don't relax.

✸ Appearance is a priority.

✸ Appear to others as the perfect family.

✸ Strive for perfection.

✸ Winning is everything.

✸ Never show weakness.

✸ You are only as good as your achievements.

✸ Feeling good about yourself means you are conceited and arrogant.

Think about what it is like for you, or what it was like for you, growing up in your family.

_____

_____

_____

_____

What are the rules in your family?

_____

_____

_____

_____

What messages do these rules send?

_____

_____

_____

_____

What impact does this have on you?

_____

_____

_____

_____

Family Boundaries

Healthy boundaries between members include respecting each member's personal space and property, privacy, and roles. Boundaries that are healthy provide a safe, nurturing environment that allows you to maintain yourself as an individual separate from your family and can contribute to feelings of independence and autonomy. Separation and independence need to be balanced with belonging to and functioning as a family. In some families, however, boundaries are inappropriate and unhealthy and can contribute to confusion, guilt, low self-esteem, lack of confidence, and bulimic symptoms.

Blurring of Roles

When family roles are not respected or are blurred, responsibilities become unclear and individuals can feel confused and uncomfortable. For example, it is important to maintain the distinction between the roles of parent, peer, and child. When parents involve their children in parental conflict, children can feel like they are being asked to choose between parents, or that somehow it is their fault that their parents are not getting along. Similarly, when parents treat their children as confidants or peers, children can end up feeling like they are responsible for their parents' happiness or well-being. In some cases, the caretaking role is completely reversed and the child ends up parenting the parent. In some families, boundaries and roles are completely disregarded and children are emotionally, physically, or sexually abused. Take some time to think about the roles in your family when you were growing up and currently.

What were the roles like in your family?

_____

_____

_____

_____

What was your role in your family?

_____

_____

Was there any role confusion? If so, what impact did this have on you?

_____

_____

_____

_____

Invasion of Privacy

It is also important that each family member's privacy is respected. Personal space, property, and time should be allowed and respected. For example, Joanne described an incident where her mother found and read her diary when she was sixteen years old. This was an ongoing concern for Joanne because she often found her mother in her room going through her things. She remembers feeling completely invaded and out of control. After this invasion, she stopped writing in her journal, despite the fact that she used her journal to sort out her thoughts and feelings. Even though Joanne knew that her mother was worried about her eating disorder and was trying to help, Joanne's bulimia intensified after this event.

In Joanne's case, lack of privacy was a problem. On the other hand, too much privacy can also be problematic because this can leave you feeling alone and without support.

What was the privacy like in your family? Was there too much or too little? What impact did it have on you?

Lack of Autonomy

Allowing individuals to accomplish tasks and make decisions on their own fosters competence and confidence. Adolescence is a natural time when the decision-making process is transferred from parents to children, and autonomy and independence starts to develop. However, this transition is not always smooth and may be difficult for some individuals and families. Your parents may have struggled to find a balance between guidance and safety, and allowing you to make your own decisions. If this process was drawn out too long, you may have felt you were not trusted or competent. Or you may have found this process too quick and felt abandoned and alone. Think back to your adolescence and reflect on what this transition was like for you.

What struggles did you encounter through adolescence?

_____

_____

What type of parental guidance did you experience? Did you feel like you had too much or too little guidance?

_____

_____

_____

_____

What were your thoughts and feelings during adolescence?

_____

_____

_____

_____

Family Involvement

Family involvement usually falls on a continuum somewhere between over-involvement and underinvolvement. Some families are enmeshed; this is where family members are overly involved in one another's lives (Minuchin el al. 1975). Enmeshment includes extreme forms of intimacy, in which parents may speak for their children because they believe they know exactly how they feel, or children may decide not to move out on their own because they worry about a parent being lonely. Enmeshment can also involve parents being overly protective and being prone to rescue their children rather than let them sort out a difficult situation on their own. For example, Dylan remembers that his parents always bailed him out with his homework. School assignments became a family project if they were due the next day and Dylan had not started his work. As a result, he never learned the skills of self-discipline and time management.

On the other end of the continuum are families that are distant, absent, or under-involved. In this type of family, you are left on your own with little guidance, rules, or support. This might be a result of stress or burnout within the family, or this might be just the way your family functions. What was the involvement like in your family? Were members overinvolved or underinvolved? What impact did this have on you?

_____

_____

_____

_____

_____

Substance Abuse

Substance abuse can have a serious impact on the family. When a family member is abusing alcohol or drugs, it can cause uncertainty and chaos within the family. You never know when the trouble will begin. For example, Terri described her situation at home with her alcoholic mother. She remembers not being able to bring a friend home from school because she never knew what state her mother would be in. Either she would be sober and fine, or she would be drunk, obnoxious and verbally abusive. Terri tried to keep the house clean and free of problems, in an attempt to prevent her mother from drinking. But no matter what she did, Teri could not control her mother's drinking or her temper. For Terri, the only way she could exert control in her life was to control her own eating and weight, and consequently, she developed bulimia.

Is someone in your household abusing alcohol or drugs?

_____

_____

What is the impact on the family?

_____

_____

_____

_____

What is the impact on you?

_____

_____

_____

_____

Family Support

Some people are lucky enough to have supportive family members and friends to help them with their recovery. This is not the case for everyone. Some loved ones may try to be supportive, but may in fact be more harmful than helpful because they don't know what to say or do. For example, comments like "you look healthy" or "are you sure you should be eating that?" may have the intention of being supportive but can be easily misinterpreted as "you are fat and eat like a pig." Be prepared for comments and questions, and ask yourself what the other person is intending to say. Do not let your eating disorder thoughts take over and convince you that you are being criticized.

Some family members and friends will not understand or want to be involved in your recovery at all. Others may have gotten used to their role as your caretaker or decision maker and may feel threatened by your attempts to improve yourself. Be prepared for the dynamic in your family to shift.

Who Can Support You Best?

Think about the people in your life who may be best able to support you in your recovery. You can think about each person individually and use the following questionnaire to evaluate how helpful this person might be.

1. To what extent does this individual have good listening skills?

   1=not at all   2=somewhat   3=extremely

2. To what extent do you think this individual is able to validate your feelings?

   1=not at all   2=somewhat   3=extremely

3. To what extent is this person critical of you?

   1=extremely   2=somewhat   3=not at all

4. To what extent does this person take your eating problems and symptoms personally?

   1=extremely   2=somewhat   3=not at all

5. How comfortable would you feel discussing your concerns with this person even if things aren't going so well?

   1=not at all   2=somewhat   3=extremely

6. Does this person stand to lose anything, or will they feel threatened if you recover?

   1=yes   2=possibly   3=no

7. Has this person ever used personal information that you have shared with him or her against you or to hurt you in anyway?

           1=yes   2=possibly   3=no

8. How often is this person available to you?

  1=not very often   2=often enough   3=all the time

Below are guidelines that you may use to help you to decide who you can ask for support. They are only guidelines, however. If you have a strong feeling about someone and how supportive he or she will be, you may want to go with your gut instinct despite his or her score.

Score 19 to 24: You are lucky to have such a supportive person in your life, and if you haven't already told this person about your bulimia, you should seriously consider sharing your struggles with this person and asking for his or her help in your recovery.

Score 14 to 18: It is not clear whether you should count on this person for support. It is possible that this person is too emotionally involved in your eating disorder, which could cause further problems. This does not mean you should rule this person out, in terms of support, but you should tread carefully and consider looking at other options.

Score 8 to 13: Unfortunately, this is a person who will not be much help to you in your recovery process. If possible, you should look for someone else who can offer you support during this difficult time. If this is not an option, it is better to work on your recovery alone than to have to deal with the frustrations involved in feeling judged or unsupported.

No More Secrets

On the one hand, your eating disorder is your business and you have the right to your privacy (of course, this depends on your age and the seriousness of your condition). You are under no obligation to tell people that you are either suffering or recovering from bulimia. In fact, it might make sense for you to decide not to share this information with coworkers or with acquaintances and extended family who you know are generally not supportive or helpful. On the other hand, bulimia does have a tendency to go underground, and if you are trying to keep it a secret, you may not be receiving the support that is available to you from your family and friends. Also, the nature of the illness fosters a great deal of deception and secrecy. You might have found yourself saying that you have already eaten when you haven't, canceling arrangements with friends and family so you can binge, and lying about symptoms. Deceiving people you love and care about can make you feel badly about yourself and fuel your eating disorder. Secrets can also intensify any shame that you might be experiencing related to the eating disorder. Consider whether you could be open and honest about your struggle with bulimia to those you care about and especially those who have the capacity to support you in your recovery.

You may be afraid of disappointing your loved ones, breaking their hearts, adding stress to their life, or you may feel embarrassed or ashamed. Try not to let your discomfort or embarrassment about your bulimia interfere with reaching out for support. One way to think about this is to ask yourself the question, "If my loved one were struggling with a serious problem, would I want them to tell me?"

You also may want to keep this information to yourself because you think that your family members or friends will not be supportive or they won't understand. If so, try to examine the evidence to determine if this is indeed true. From past experiences, you may know that you are going to have a bigger problem on your hands if you share your concerns with certain people. On the other hand, you may have some fears that are unfounded, and it may be worth the risk to let people into your life, especially if they can provide some relief or support. One possibility is to find a family therapist who can help you tell your family and help to process any reactions and concerns. Chapter 13 reviews ways to find professional help.

Also, keep in mind that your family and friends may want to share this information about your eating disorder with other people. This can be difficult for you, especially if you have kept your eating disorder a secret. Although your loved ones have the right to share this information in order to obtain their own support, you can ask them to be discreet and also to let you know who they have told about your eating disorder.

How to Tell Your Loved Ones

When you decide to tell loved ones about your bulimia, treat it as you would any serious issue. Make sure that there is enough time available and that neither of you will have to rush off. You may even want to book some time in advance by asking when they are available to spend some time with you to discuss an important issue. Then, don't beat around the bush. Let the person know that you have been struggling with bulimia for however long your struggle has been.

You may need to educate loved ones about bulimia by telling them about your symptoms and your feelings about yourself. Also tell them where you are, in terms of your stage of recovery. Let them know why you didn't tell them before (you were embarrassed, you thought you could handle it yourself, or you didn't want to worry them) and why you have decided to tell them now (you need their help, you are tired of lying about it, or you have decided to work on recovery). Give them a chance to process the information, ask questions, and react to the information.

Coping with Reactions

Family members and friends may react in many ways to finding out about your eating disorder. Some of these reactions are described below.

* **"I knew it all along."** You might be surprised or not surprised to find out that this is not new information, and that family members or friends have suspected or known about your bulimia for some time. They may have been struggling with themselves to figure out a way to approach you, or they may have tried to speak to you in the past and been brushed off or sent a message to back off.

* **"How can I help?"** This is a good reaction. Your loved ones are showing genuine concern and want to know how they can help you with your recovery from bulimia. It means they want to take the time to listen to your concerns and struggles and work with you to make plans to support you.

* **"I'll take care of everything."** This reaction is when your loved ones want to try to take control and fix your bulimia. It could involve insisting that you get treatment or monitoring your eating and symptoms. Since no one else can really fix your bulimia, this is the time to speak up about what you would find helpful and what might be unhelpful.

* **"Snap out of it."** Otherwise known as the "just eat" reaction. Some people will not understand the complexity of bulimia, and will also have certain beliefs about how to conquer problems that entail pulling yourself up by your bootstraps and using your willpower. This is usually not helpful. If it really were just a matter of willpower, you would have solved this problem on your own, ages ago. Unfortunately, willpower is not enough to fight bulimic urges and to recover from bulimia. Educating your loved ones about eating disorders, such as having them read the first few chapters in this book, might help to soften this reaction.

* **"How could this happen?"** Be aware that loved ones may react defensively. They may worry about being blamed for the eating disorder or become concerned about how this news will reflect on them or the family. This reaction may be based on feelings of anger, guilt, or fear. If you do get a defensive reaction, be aware that it has the potential to shift into a more supportive response, once the individual has time to process the information.

What Others Can Do to Help

Once you have identified and recruited some support, it is time to figure out what your family and friends can do to help. First of all, it can be a huge relief to you to be open and honest with someone you care about. Sometimes this is enough to reduce some of the stress in your life so that you can direct your energy toward your recovery. Ideally, a supportive person is available to you when you want to talk, and can listen and let you express your feelings without being critical or judgmental. When people know about your bulimia, it is also easier to recruit them for strategies that you can use to avoid acting on urges for symptoms. For example, once Jan's mother knew about her bulimia, she tried to make herself available to join Jan for a leisurely walk or a game of cards after dinner. This helped to prevent Jan from vomiting.

Although it is great to have support, it is important that you continue to take responsibility for your eating and your recovery. Otherwise, well-intentioned support can backfire and cause you to feel like you are not in control. It is common for loved ones not to know how to be supportive without overdoing it, so you may want to give them some guidance. One way to provide guidance is to coach your loved ones on what is helpful and what is not. For example, you can tell them that it is helpful if they join you for a meal, but comments about what you are eating or your appearance are not helpful. If you think that your friends and family are open to suggestions on how best to offer you support, you may want to ask them to read the guide for family members and friends that follows this section, at the end of this chapter.

Remember, your role is to ask for what you want, and to help your family members and friends help you. But remember that no one is perfect. Just because you ask for what you need in terms of support does not guarantee that you are going to get it. Try not to be critical of those who cannot or won't comply with your requests. Determine what kind of support is available to you, and use it to your advantage, even if it isn't ideal. Finally, it is important to keep in mind that people can recover without any support at all.

A Guide for Family Members and Friends

Here are some dos and don'ts for family members and friends. It is important to

* **Educate yourself about bulimia.** Bulimia develops and is maintained by a combination of factors, and bulimic symptoms can serve as a very effective coping mechanism. Once the bulimic cycle is activated, it is very difficult to break. Your loved one cannot "snap out of it" or use will power to overcome bulimia.

* **Compliment and reinforce characteristics and interests other than weight and appearance.** Part of recovery for your loved one is to separate his or her self-esteem from appearance. You can help by commenting on strengths, abilities, and interests that are not related to appearance, weight, or shape.

🌼 **Share activities that don't raise concerns about weight and shape.** This can also help your loved one to learn to obtain self-worth from areas not related to weight and shape, and at the same time provide a distraction from urges to have symptoms.

🌼 **Express your concerns, and communicate directly and openly.** Don't beat around the bush. If you have concerns, it is good to express them directly. This models good communication for your loved one and also helps you to avoid sending indirect and confusing messages.

🌼 **Offer your support by being available and listening.** Use your listening skills and allow your loved one to talk about what is on his or her mind. Try not to offer advice or to fix things.

🌼 **Be open to letting your loved one talk about his or her feelings.** Part of your loved one's recovery from bulimia includes identifying and expressing feelings.

🌼 **Allow your loved one to be independent and in charge of his or her own recovery.** It is important that your loved one start to build up his or her level of confidence, in order to recover from bulimia. To support this process, you will need to keep a balance between offering support and allowing your loved one to accomplish tasks and make decisions on his or her own.

🌼 **Realize that it is best for your loved one to go at his or her own pace and make his or her own decisions in terms of eating and recovery.** If your loved one feels coerced, your attempts to help could backfire.

🌼 **Examine your own beliefs about food, weight, and shape.** Your beliefs about eating, your own weight, or other people's weight may be contrary to the approach your loved one needs. It is helpful to examine your beliefs and to be aware of any direct or indirect messages that you might be sending.

🌼 **Treat your loved one like any other family member or friend.** If you give your loved one special status because of the eating disorder, you may inadvertently reinforce the bulimia.

🌼 **Encourage professional help if needed.** Or, if your loved one has decided to discuss his or her problems outside the family, support this decision.

🌼 **Be aware of your own and other family members' needs.** Bulimia can take a serious toll on a family or a friendship. Try to take care of yourself and find ways of obtaining support for yourself.

🌼 **Be patient.** Recovery may take some time. Having symptom slips after a symptom-free period is not unusual and does not mean your loved one is giving up or is back to square one.

The following is a list of don'ts.

- **Don't comment on weight, shape, or appearance.** Any comment that you make about weight, shape, or appearance will probably be interpreted negatively. It also sends the message that your loved one's appearance or body size is important to you. Avoid making comments even if your loved one asks for your opinion. In this case, you might want to refer to this guideline, and state that you don't want to go there because you think that it is not in his or her best interest.

- **Don't ignore the problem.** Bulimia is a complex problem that usually doesn't go away on its own. Your loved one will benefit from your understanding and support.

- **Don't blame yourself or your loved one for the eating disorder.** Blaming will not help the situation and will likely leave you feeling guilty or angry.

- **Don't demand change.** If it were easy to change and recover from bulimia, then your loved one would have already done so. Your loved one has a difficult battle ahead and can benefit from your patience.

- **Don't get involved in a power struggle.** This is the last place you want to be. This will give the eating disorder strength and power. If you find that you are involved in a discussion or a dynamic where your loved one is arguing in favor of the eating disorder and you are arguing the other side, disengage and reevaluate.

- **Don't take control or police eating or symptoms.** This may lead your loved one to feel out of control.

- **Don't rescue your loved one.** This can lead to feelings of ineffectiveness, incompetence, and dependence.

- **Don't give the eating disorder special status.** This type of attention can reinforce the eating disorder and make it difficult for your loved one to recover.

- **Don't take on the role of a therapist.** Know your limits and recognize your own needs.

Note: There may be exceptions to these guidelines based on the seriousness of your loved one's condition and his or her age. For example, sometimes it is necessary to take control or to rescue your loved one if their life is in danger or they are very young.

Chapter 12

Avoiding the Slippery
Slope of Relapse

As you know, an eating disorder involves a variety of thoughts and behaviors that are very resistant to change. Although the road to recovery from bulimia is a long and difficult journey, it is possible to recover. Hopefully, with the help of this book, you have been able to make some changes to your symptoms and your eating disorder thoughts. It is not uncommon to find that your behavioral symptoms have changed but your thoughts continue to be problematic. For example, one eating disorder thought that may persist is the belief that your self-worth is reliant on your weight and shape. As a result, it becomes tempting to resort back to eating disorder behaviors during times of stress and when you feel badly about yourself. In addition, you may have a number of underlying issues that do not feel resolved, or new concerns may be beginning to surface. Many people report that this is the time when they feel worse than ever. Normal eating and symptom control are an important first step in your journey, but in some ways this is just the beginning of your recovery.

For some time after you have managed to interrupt your bulimic symptoms, you are at serious risk of relapsing. Georgia, who has been in treatment for her eating disorder on and off for the past five years, described the process of making changes to her bulimia as climbing up a very steep and rocky mountain. Forward movement is slow, arduous, and unpredictable, and the transition from working on symptom control to being symptomatic is as easy as sliding down a very slippery slope. To prevent relapse, it is important to continue using strategies to avoid symptoms, challenging your eating disorder thoughts, and working on your underlying issues.

Sticking to the Experiment

One helpful notion is to remind yourself of the experimental nature of maintaining your recovery from bulimia. You know what it is like to live with an eating disorder. Maintaining your eating and working toward being symptom-free will give you a sense of what it is like to live without an eating disorder. If you decide that your life was better or more tolerable with bulimia, then you can always go back to dieting and/or the eating disorder. This is always an option that is open to you. But don't decide to return to the eating disorder prematurely. You need to give yourself a chance to get through the difficult times and to experience some of the benefits of recovery. Usually you need to give yourself a full year or longer of recovery. After enough time has passed and you know what it is like to live without bulimia, you can make an educated decision about how you want to live your life: with or without an eating disorder.

Knowing What to Expect

During recovery, you may experience periods when you feel more preoccupied with food, more dissatisfied with your body image, more anxious and depressed, and you feel strong urges for symptoms. Some say it is like hitting a brick wall, and many report that it is easier to engage in symptoms at this point than to experience the intense distress associated with symptom management. You might believe that you were much better off when you were active with your eating disorder, and you may be tempted to relapse at this point. This is not a good time to decide to go back to the eating disorder. Use your strategies to avoid acting on these urges, and try to work through the distress. Sometimes it is helpful to put off your decision to have symptoms for one day or one week. After this time, when you are not so stressed, you can re-evaluate your situation.

We are not suggesting that life without an eating disorder will ever be perfect and problem-free. In fact, without your bulimia as a coping mechanism, you may find yourself faced with more stress, at least until you develop other coping skills. And even after you have developed more adaptive coping methods, you will still be exposed to the hassles, problems, disappointments, and tragedies that are part of the human experience. The difference is that without the physical and psychological complications associated with bulimia you will be more equipped to deal with these stressors.

Exploring Past Relapses

If this is not your first attempt at recovery, it can be extremely helpful to explore what sent you down the slippery slope of relapse in the past. It is helpful to analyze these past experiences and to try to identify factors that contributed to your relapse so that you can prevent it from happening again. It is important not to dwell on past relapses as personal failures because this will interfere with your strength and motivation to recover. Rather, try to utilize your experience with past relapses as a valuable learning opportunity. Remember, each time you try to make a change to your bulimia, you can build on your past experience with recovery to increase the chances of long-term permanent change. Use the Exploring Past Relapses Worksheet to help you with this task. If this is your first attempt to change, then skip the worksheet and continue with the next section.

Exploring Past Relapses Worksheet

When was your last attempt to change your bulimic behaviors and thoughts?

_____

_____

_____

What changes did you make?

_____

_____

_____

How long did the changes last?

_____

_____

What were the factors that led to a recurrence of symptoms?

_____

_____

_____

_____

What did you learn from this attempt to change?

_____

_____

_____

_____

How can you prepare to deal with these factors this time around?

_____

_____

_____

_____

Reminding Yourself of Your Progress

If you are frustrated because you are still struggling with your eating disorder thoughts, urges, and some symptoms, it is helpful to remind yourself of the progress that you have made so far. It is best to evaluate your progress over a reasonable amount of time. For example, if you have just binged or vomited, it is not helpful to evaluate yourself based on the events of the day, but rather to reflect on a longer time period. Think back to one week ago, one month ago, six months ago, or one year ago. Think about where you were in terms of your bulimic symptoms and thoughts, and compare this to where you are now. You may have made significant changes to your symptoms and may even have been abstinent from symptoms altogether, or you may still be struggling with symptoms. Even if you are still symptomatic, you might have reduced your bingeing, had breakfast for the first time, used a strategy, or begun to challenge some of your eating disorder thoughts. Just considering recovery represents an important step. It is essential to take credit for any progress that you have made, no matter how large or small the change. Although this book may have given you some ideas and pointed you in a direction, it is your hard work that is responsible for any changes that you have made to your behavior or thinking.

Identifying and Challenging Thought Distortions

In chapter 6, we covered the role that thought distortions play in your eating disorder. There are also thought distortions that are relevant to relapse prevention—ways of perceiving and interpreting your situation that increase the likelihood of slipping down the slippery slope of relapse. For example, you may have a tendency to see your recovery as all or nothing: "I am either recovering or relapsing," or "I binged last night, so I'm back to square one". These thoughts are problematic because if you are not perfectly symptom free, then you see yourself as relapsing. This type of thinking does not leave room for mistakes or setbacks in recovery, and can therefore set you up for an actual relapse that could have been avoided. If a symptom is interpreted as representing relapse, then one symptom can easily lead to another (Marlatt and Gordon 1985). The thought process goes, "Why not binge? I have already screwed up, and have to start from scratch anyway." In addiction literature, this is called the "abstinence violation effect" (Marlatt and Rohsenow 1980, p. 159). One way to avoid the abstinence violation effect is to remind yourself that setbacks are a normal part of recovery. Just because you have acted on urges or have experienced a setback does not put you back to square one or erase all of your hard work. Recovery is not an absolute. Rather, there are different degrees of recovery, and it is okay and expected that you will experience setbacks on your journey.

Also, be on the lookout for thought processes related to the recovery process that overgeneralize. For example, "I binged yesterday. I will never be able to control my eating. I am a total failure." If you believe that you are a total failure, then it will be very difficult, if not impossible, to get back on track and maintain your recovery. Remind yourself again that setbacks are a normal part of recovery. Yes, you may have struggled yesterday, but that does not mean that you will never be able to avoid acting on urges to binge. Furthermore, even if you did make a mistake yesterday, that does not mean that you are a failure as a person. Mistakes and weaknesses are part of the human condition, and everyone makes a mistake at one time or another. Having a setback in one area of your life does not say anything about your abilities in other areas. If you overgeneralize and perceive yourself as a total failure, this will have a very negative impact on your self-esteem and confidence and will lower the energy that you need to recover. See the setback for what it is, and move on.

Similarly, thoughts that catastrophize the situation can also interfere with the recovery process. Consider this line of thinking by Stephen, who is a corporate lawyer. "I had a strong urge to vomit at work because I was so stressed. I can't deal with urges like that everyday. I have no choice but to quit my job. I won't be able to support myself. I will end up out on the street." Although it is a pretty big jump from urges to vomit to being homeless, it took Stephen less than five seconds to get there. It is important to slow down this thinking process and to introduce more realistic and balanced thoughts. The truth is that Stephen can deal with strong urges to vomit; in fact, he has been doing it for eight months. And yes, it would be very difficult to deal with these urges every day, but in reality, Stephen's intense urges only occur after he receives negative feedback from his superior. One option is to quit his job, but this is not his only choice. He could decide to speak to his superior about his difficulties, he could decide to continue to use strategies to manage the urges to vomit, he could work on why it is so hard for him to receive criticism, or he could ask for a transfer. Even if he did decide to quit his job, he could find another job to support himself. In fact, the chances of him ending up on the street and homeless are very small.

You can use the Shifting Problematic Thoughts Worksheet from chapter 5 to help you to identify and challenge these thoughts as you try to maintain your recovery.

Slips

A slip is not the same as a relapse. When you act on an urge for a symptom, usually in response to a risky situation, it is a slip. Slips are a normal part of recovery. A slip does not erase all your hard work. Still, it is important to protect against slips because they can make you more vulnerable.

Avoiding Slips

The best way to protect against slips is to avoid or plan for high-risk situations. Risky situations include:

* pressures to control your weight

* unpleasant emotions such as anxiety or depression

* pleasant emotions, such as wanting to celebrate

* physical discomfort, such as feeling hungry or full

* being alone and having the opportunity to have symptoms

* conflict with others

* certain types of food

* habitual settings

* feeling fat

* unintentional changes in weight/eating habits

* a change of season.

Consider this example. Julie had been working on her recovery from bulimia for fourteen months, and she was eating a well-balanced and nutritious meal plan and had not binged or vomited for six months. Although she wasn't satisfied with her body, she was tolerating it and not attempting to change it. On the advice of her dentist, she decided to have her wisdom teeth removed. Due to the pain involved and her inability to chew, she went on a liquid diet for a few days. As a result she lost a couple of pounds and felt pretty good about herself. She was reminded of what it was like to restrict her eating and to lose weight, and it felt great. This set off a new diet and exercise regime, and it wasn't long before she was bingeing and vomiting again.

Other situations that might unintentionally affect your eating or weight and activate the bulimic cycle include illness, being busy, or traveling.

If you have been working on your recovery and you are feeling like you can at least tolerate your body, you should know that this is much easier to do during the colder months. During this time you are covered up with long pants, sweaters and jackets, and your body image is less of an issue and is less likely to trigger your negative body image thoughts and feelings. It is a whole new ball game when the weather starts to warm up, or you take a warm weather vacation and you are wearing T-shirts, shorts, and bathing suits. Do not be surprised if your urges to diet and exercise start to increase during this time. Try to remind yourself that engaging in this behavior will likely lead to other bulimic symptoms, and try to spend some time learning to tolerate your body again.

Avoiding Stressors

You may also act on an urge for a symptom in response to stressors. Stressors are different from risky situations as they are ongoing and cumulative. Stressors include but are not limited to marital or relationship difficulties, personal or family illnesses, lack of time, work or school duties, parenting, financial situations, moving, and daily hassles. Stressors have a way of adding up and depleting your energy and affecting your mood. In the past, you may have responded to stressors by having symptoms, in an attempt to relieve stress or improve your mood. Now it is important that you learn to cope with stressors in a more adaptive and healthy way.

You may be able to relax by doing such things as getting together with friends, by going out to see a movie or a play, listening to or creating music, playing sports, taking a yoga class, going to church, taking a vacation, taking a long bath, meditating, walking, being involved in nature, writing poems, creating art, gardening, golfing, reading, watching television, sailing, spending time with pets or animals, doing crafts, or shopping. In order to maximize your mental health and reduce the likelihood of slips and relapse, it is important to identify what helps you to relax and take time to do it. What works for you when it comes to relaxing? If you don't know, what would you be willing to try?

1. _____

2. _____

3. _____

Dealing with Slips

After a slip, it is important to get back on track immediately, the sooner the better. For example, if you skip breakfast, then have a normal lunch. If you binge at lunch, have a normal dinner. If you vomit dinner, try to replace that dinner as soon as possible. That's right, have another dinner and use strategies to keep it down. Waiting for the next day or the next Monday to get back on track can set you up for more symptoms and start the slide toward relapse. Although slips can be very upsetting, it is possible to consider them as a temporary setback and a valuable learning experience. You should take the time to analyze the slip to determine what the triggers were, and to think about alternative courses of action other than acting on urges for symptoms. With this information, you can plan carefully what to do if you encounter the same situation again. Ask yourself these questions:

✹ What symptoms were involved in the slip?

✹ What unhelpful thoughts were present?

✳ What statements or facts might help to shift your unhelpful thoughts to a more realistic view?

✳ What are the factors that contributed to the slip?

✳ What stressors were present (ongoing stress in your life)?

✳ What can you learn from this slip?

✳ What can you do differently in the future to avoid further slips?

No matter how far along you are in your recovery, if you have a slip it is important to return to strategies that you used in the earlier stages of your recovery. In other words, go back to basics. Some people find that returning to mechanical eating and treating food as medicine are extremely helpful in the face of trying to get back on track after a slip. Others return to recording their meals and urges in a journal, and using strategies such as distraction to avoid acting on urges for symptoms.

Ask yourself what you need to do differently in terms of your eating and meal planning. What do you need to do to prevent other symptoms? Do you need to work on your thoughts about your weight and body? Do you need to work on your social support? Develop a plan of action to get back on track. You can always reevaluate the plan and make changes to improve upon it.

Finally, here are some tips for dealing with slips:

✳ Be prepared for their arrival.

✳ Label them appropriately (slip versus relapse).

✳ Get back on track immediately.

✳ Return to concrete strategies.

✳ Challenge your problematic thinking.

✳ Remind yourself of your progress.

✳ Use slips as learning experiences.

✳ Remember that recovery takes time.

Continuing to Build Your Self-Esteem

An important part of relapse prevention is to continue your work on developing a sense of self-worth that is separate from the eating disorder and separate from weight and shape. Remind yourself about your values, interests, and long-term goals. Remember to make an effort to become involved in activities that are not connected to weight and shape, and continue to challenge your beliefs in this area.

Working on Underlying Issues

Many people find that as they recover from an eating disorder, and issues of food and weight become less evident and time-consuming, they are left with many of the issues that may have triggered the bulimia in the first place. Underlying problems may include issues related to self-esteem, abandonment, relationships, sexual or physical abuse, perfectionism, expectations, fear of failure or the future, and body image.

You may want to find professional help to deal with your issues. Chapter 13 discusses various therapy options.

Processing underlying issues is an important part of the recovery process, but be prepared for the possibility that it will trigger intense thoughts and feelings that can lead to relapse. Be prepared for strong urges as you begin or continue to process underlying issues and concerns. Work on underlying issues should proceed at a slow, manageable pace; the idea is to regulate this stressful work so that it does not disrupt your healthy eating.

Don't Give Up

An eating disorder does not develop overnight. Likewise, it will not disappear overnight. Recovery from an eating disorder takes time and should be viewed as a long-term goal. Be patient with yourself and give yourself lots of time to do this work. Remember, you will likely feel worse before you feel better, and at times the urges to have symptoms will be powerful. Expect to struggle with bulimic urges and thoughts for some time even after you have normalized your eating. Make sure that you are both physically and psychologically satisfied with respect to your eating, and use your coping strategies to guide you through this journey. No matter how many times you slip, use the strategies in this book and in this chapter to get back on track with your recovery. Finally, keep in mind this advice from a woman who struggled with bulimia for over a decade before she was able to recover: "Don't give up. The path will take you in all different directions, but it's worth it. Feel the feelings and expect to slip. No matter how long it takes, you're better off in recovery than you are in the throes of bulimia."

Chapter 13

Getting Additional Help

If you have read through this book and have completed the worksheets, and you are still struggling with bulimia, don't despair. There are still steps you can take to recover. Additional treatment is available and may be necessary. This includes therapy, medication, or some combination of the two. Some people will require additional treatment in order to break the bulimia cycle, and other people will choose to obtain therapy to maintain the changes they have made and to work on underlying issues and associated problems.

Therapy

Therapy can take a number of different forms. Individual or group therapy can provide a supportive environment to work on your eating disorder symptoms and your underlying issues. Family therapy can provide an opportunity to involve your family in your recovery, and to address issues and dynamics within your family or relationships. In order to find appropriate therapy, you may want to start by asking your family doctor for a referral. Often physicians will have resources that you may not have access to. You can also look for eating disorder programs in your area or contact your national eating disorder information representative. In the United States you can contact the National Eating Disorder

Association (www.nationaleatingdisorders.org), in Canada you can contact the National Eating Disorder Information Centre (www.nedic.ca), and in the United Kingdom you can contact the Eating Disorders Association Resource Centre (www .uq.net.au/eda/documents/start.html). These centers will have a list of eating disorder resources, services, and therapists that are available in your area. Cost will depend on where you live, your access to insurance, and what service you utilize. Some therapists will operate on a sliding scale and may be able to reduce their rates to accommodate your budget. Be sure to ask about cost and if there is a waiting period when you are exploring your options.

Individual Therapy

If you decide that you would like to try to work on your issues with a therapist on a one-to-one basis, than you need to pursue individual therapy. The main advantages of individual therapy are that you will have the entire time allotted to work on your own issues, your privacy is better protected, and you can usually negotiate with your therapist to schedule appointments that are convenient for you. For example, you may decide that you prefer to have appointments early in the morning so that you can get to work, or you may decide that certain days are better for you than other days. Usually, individual therapy occurs weekly, but you can negotiate with your therapist to meet twice a week, every other week, or monthly, whatever will work best for you. Sessions usually last between forty-five minutes and one hour.

It is important that you and your therapist are a good match, and that you feel you can work well together. This includes feeling comfortable with your therapist and understanding and agreeing with the therapist's approach. For example, some therapists will take a cognitive-behavioral approach (like the one that is described in this book), whereas other therapists may take a more insight-oriented approach that includes exploring your childhood or your current relationships. Depending on your needs, you may choose one approach over another. For example, if you are still struggling with eating disorder thoughts and symptoms, you may want to work with someone who will continue with the cognitive behavioral work that you started by reading this book. On the other hand, if you are ready to move beyond symptom control and start to process underlying issues, you may be looking for another approach. Keep in mind that most therapists usually use a combination of different approaches.

You also may want to consider expertise. If you are struggling with depression, you may want to work with someone who has experience with eating disorders and depression, or if you have a history of sexual abuse, you may want to work with someone who has experience in treating trauma. Sometimes, finding a therapist requires shopping around and interviewing a number of people before making your decision about who to work with.

Group Therapy

There are advantages to group therapy over individual therapy. For one, there is usually less of a wait, and if there is a fee for service, group therapy is cheaper than individual therapy. Other advantages include what you get from the group that you cannot get from individual therapy. This includes connecting with people who are struggling with some of the same things that you are, feeling like you are not alone or crazy, learning from and interacting with other group members, and feeling good because you have been able to support or help others.

Groups can take a variety of different forms, and you should investigate this carefully. Some groups follow a closed format, meaning that there is a specific beginning and ending date. All group members start at the same time and finish together. No new members will join part way through. These groups tend to have a structured agenda for each session. Other groups follow an open format, meaning that people will start and finish at different times throughout the group's lifespan. Open groups are often less structured as well. Attendance can range from being mandatory to being more flexible. Usually a group will meet once a week for one to two hours and, on average, consist of eight to ten people.

The focus of the group is also important. Groups can focus on symptom interruption, psychoeducation, motivation, nutrition, body image, relapse prevention, interpersonal relations, grief, abuse, anxiety, and so on. Depending on the group, there also may be certain restrictions based on age, gender, weight, or symptom level. It is important to meet the facilitators of the group, have a chance to ask questions about their approach and the group, and to feel that a group is a good match for you.

Day Hospital

If you are having trouble breaking the bulimia cycle and you are still bingeing, purging, and restricting on a regular basis, then you may need intensive treatment. As you know, the bulimia has a way of taking on a life of its own, and try as you might, you may not be able to fight urges to binge and purge. Or, despite the education in this book about how important it is to eat normally, you may still find it impossible to eat a piece of cake and keep it down. If this is the case, you should talk to your doctor about intensive treatment. One type of intensive treatment is outpatient, or day hospital, treatment. This means coming for the day several days per week but going home each night. The idea is to provide a safe environment where you can learn to eat normally and control your symptoms.

Although every day hospital is a little different, we will describe one example to give you a sense of what is involved. The Toronto Hospital Day Hospital runs five days per week (Monday to Friday) from approximately 10:00 A.M. to 6:30 P.M. The program runs from six to eight weeks. Each day involves group therapy and supervised meals. Group topics include body image, nutrition, psychoeducation, assertiveness training, self-esteem, relationships, and coping strategies. Patients are given a meal plan that incorporates normal eating, and they are provided with lunch, afternoon snack, and dinner. Patients are expected to have breakfast outside of program time. After meals, patients remain on the unit and do not have access to washrooms.

Patients are encouraged to talk about urges for symptoms and feelings that arise when they do not act on these urges. Staff and other group members provide support. Eventually, patients learn that urges subside and that they can survive without acting on them. In other words, the bulimia cycle is interrupted. Once the process is started, patients learn to transfer this ability to fight urges outside of the program.

Inpatient Treatment

Some people cannot break the bulimia cycle without constant support in the initial stages and these people require inpatient treatment. Inpatient programs involve staying in the hospital twenty-four hours per day for several weeks. In some programs patients go home for weekends after the first few weeks and/or may graduate to day attendance partway through treatment.

In some areas, day hospital treatment may not be available, so inpatient treatment may be the only option.

Medications

Another treatment option that you may want to consider, in combination with this book or therapy, is medication. While medication alone is often not enough to provide long-term recovery from bulimia, it can be part of your treatment plan. Medication may be able to provide additional relief that will increase your ability to recover.

There are medications available that can help to reduce urges to binge, and medications that reduce the stomach pain and bloating associated with the initial stages of normal eating. There are also medications that can treat problems that commonly occur in the context of bulimia such as depression, anxiety, and insomnia (Molleken 2000). If you are considering medication, it is best to discuss this with your family doctor or a psychiatrist, who can answer your questions and prescribe the medication. It is not uncommon to have fears and concerns about being on medication, and you should discuss your concerns, if you have any.

Antidepressants

For many people with bulimia, antidepressant medication can help to decrease urges to binge and episodes of binge eating. Even if you are not depressed, antidepressants may help reduce your urges to binge. Of course, if you are also struggling with symptoms of depression and/or anxiety, an antidepressant will target these conditions as well. There are several different classes of antidepressants, and all appear to decrease bingeing. Currently, the serotonergic reuptake inhibitors (SSRIs), such as fluoxetine, fluvoxamine, paroxetine, sertraline, and citalopram, are almost always considered first, because they are safer and associated with fewer side effects. SSRIs have been shown to be effective for bulimia, depression, panic disorder, and obsessive-compulsive disorder. All of these conditions have been associated with an imbalance of serotonin in the brain. It is likely that the SSRIs help to correct this imbalance and therefore reduce symptoms (Mollekin 2000).

A major study on the treatment of bulimia showed that an SSRI reduced bingeing and purging, concerns about weight and shape, and depression and anxiety symptoms (Fluoxetine Bulimia Nervosa Collaborative Study Group 1992). Overall, studies show that cognitive behavioral therapy is superior to treatment with SSRIs alone for bulimia, but that medication does add to therapy for some patients (Zhu and Walsh 2002).

If you decide to try an antidepressant, you should know that it might take up to six weeks for it to start to work. It is important that you are taking the right dose and that you are not missing dosages. Also, if you are vomiting after you take your medication, the medication will not be absorbed properly, and it will not work in the way it is intended. You should take the medication at a time of day when you are less likely to vomit. Compared with the treatment of depression, higher doses of SSRIs are required to treat bulimia. Using fluoxetine as an example, a dosage of 60 mg is generally needed and well tolerated. If you have a good response to the medication, it is recommended that you continue to take it for six months to one year before you consider discontinuing use. If you do not have a good response your doctor may try other doses or other medications to suit your needs (Mitchell and de Zwann 1993).

Potential side effects of SSRIs are agitation, insomnia, sedation, headache and sexual dysfunction. Of the SSRIs, only one, paroxetine, has been associated with weight gain and should therefore be monitored carefully in the treatment of bulimia. It is hard enough to recover from bulimia without the added stress of medication-induced weight gain. Antidepressants are not addictive, but when it is time to come off the medication, it should be tapered off slowly to avoid side effects associated with withdrawal.

Medication for Gastrointestinal Distress

Medication can help relieve distress to the gastrointestinal system, and decrease symptoms of reflux, bloating, and discomfort, especially after meals. These symptoms can make normal eating very difficult and can lead to urges to vomit, take laxatives, exercise, and/or restrict intake. Although bloating and discomfort eventually subside after you resume normal eating, domperidone can speed up your digestive system and help to ease the difficult process of eating during the initial stages. Another medication in this category is cisapride. However, cisapride is rarely prescribed anymore for bulimia because it has recently been associated with abnormal hearth rhythms that can lead to death (Molleken 2000).

Medications for Sleep Problems

Sleep problems are common in bulimia. Some people have difficulty falling asleep, others wake up numerous times throughout the evening, and others wake up very early in the morning. These problems all lead to sleep deprivation and can intensify the psychological distress and difficulties that are already triggered by the bulimia, especially anxiety, trouble concentrating, and irritability. Once you have normalized your eating and have stopped your bulimic symptoms, sleep difficulties often subside. In some cases, however, difficulties continue because insomnia is a result of underlying depression. If this is true for you, then your depression will need to be addressed before your sleep improves.

Many different medications are available for insomnia, and your doctor can help you decide which one is the best for you. Medications for insomnia should be used only in the short term. The newer ones (such as zopiclone, zolpidem) are good because they provide a sleep that is close to your natural sleep pattern, and produce less of a hung-over feeling the next morning. Over-the-counter sleep aids are not recommended as they do not provide a normal sleep pattern, and they can stop working after only a short period of use (Molleken 2000).

Treatment Recommendations

Obviously you know what is best for you when it comes to your care and treatment, and ultimately your treatment decisions are up to you. Having said that, we offer the following recommendations if you feel like you need additional treatment. If the service is available and affordable, it is a good idea to have an individual therapist. An individual therapist can provide you with the expertise and support that you need in order to get well and stay well. In general, therapy is a great way to maintain your emotional health. After you start working with an individual therapist, she or he can help you decide if more intensive treatment or group therapy might be helpful for you.

Cognitive behavioral therapy is the treatment of choice for most people recovering from bulimia. Some people will also benefit from a combination of therapy and medication. You may want to try an antidepressant if you are also suffering from depression. An antidepressant may also be helpful if you continue to feel depressed despite the fact that your eating disorder symptoms have improved.

Even if you are not depressed, an antidepressant may be helpful if you continue to struggle with your bulimic symptoms after trying the interventions that are described in this book (Mitchell and de Zwann 1993).

If you are unsure about therapy or medication, you can always try it as an experiment. If you decide not to continue with therapy, you can speak to your therapist about this and end your work at any time. Similarly, if you decide that you prefer not to be on medication, you can work with your physician to discontinue its use. On the other hand, therapy and/or medication may well provide you with the extra support you need to interrupt the bulimic cycle, maintain your recovery, and maximize your physical and emotional health.

References

American Psychiatric Association (APA). 2000. *Diagnostic and Statistical Manual of Mental Disorders.* 4th ed. Text revision. Washington, DC: American Psychiatric Publishing.

Antony, M. M., C. L. Purdon, V. Huta, and R. P. Swinson. 1998. Dimensions of perfectionism across the anxiety disorders. *Behaviour Research and Therapy* 36:1143–1154.

Antony, M. M., and R. P. Swinson. 2000. *Shyness and Social Anxiety Workbook: Proven Techniques for Overcoming Fears.* Oakland, Calif.: New Harbinger Publications.

Barlow, D. H., and M. G. Craske. 1994. *Mastery of Your Anxiety and Panic II.* San Antonio: Graywind Publications/The Psychological Corporation.

Beck, A. T. 1964. Thinking and depression: II. Theory and therapy. *Archives of General Psychiatry* 10:561–571.

———. 1976. *Cognitive Therapy and the Emotional Disorders.* New York: International Universities Press.

Beck, A. T., R. L. Greenberg, and G. Emery. 1990. *Anxiety Disorders and Phobias: A Cognitive Perspective.* New York: Basic Books.

Beck, A. T., A. J. Rush, B. F. Shaw, and G. Emery. 1979. *Cognitive Therapy of Depression.* New York: The Guilford Press.

Beck, J. S. 1995. *Cognitive Therapy: Basics and Beyond.* New York: The Guilford Press.

Bell, L., and K. Newns. 2002. What is multi-impulsive bulimia and can multi-impulsive patients benefit from supervised self-help? *European Eating Disorders Review* 10:4413–4427.

Bennett, W., and J. Gurin. 1982. *The Dieter's Dilemma: Eating Less and Weighing More*. New York: Basic Books.

Bo-Linn, G. W., C. A. Santa Ana, S. G. Morawski, and J. S. Fordtran. 1983. Purging and calorie absorption in bulimic patients and normal women. *Annals of Internal Medicine* 99:14–17.

Bourne, E. 2000. *The Anxiety and Phobia Workbook*. 3d ed. Oakland, Calif.: New Harbinger Publications.

Briere, J., and E. Gil. 1998. Self-mutilation in clinical and general population samples: Prevalence, correlates, and functions. *American Journal of Orthopsychiatry* 68:609–620.

Bulik, C. M., P. F. Sullivan, F. A. Carter, and P. R. Joyce. 1996. Lifetime anxiety disorders in women with bulimia nervosa. *Comprehensive Psychiatry* 37:368–374.

Burns, D. 1999. *The Feeling Good Handbook Revised*. New York: Penguin Books.

Cash, T. F. 1995. Developmental teasing about physical appearance: Retrospective descriptions and relationships with body image. *Social Behavior and Personality* 23:123–129.

de Zwann, M., and J. E. Mitchell. 1993. Medical complications of anorexia and bulimia nervosa. In *Medical Issues and the Eating Disorders: The Interface*, edited by A. Kaplan and P. E. Garfinkel. New York: Brunner/Mazel.

Ellis, A. 1962. *Reason and Emotion in Psychotherapy*. New York: Lyle Stuart.

Esplen, M. J., R. Gallop, and P. E. Garfinkel. 1999. Using guided imagery to enhance self-soothing in women with bulimia nervosa. *Bulletin of the Menninger Clinic* 63:174–190.

Fairburn, C. G., M. D. Marcus, and G. T. Wilson. 1993. Cognitive-behavioral therapy for binge eating and bulimia nervosa: A comprehensive treatment manual. In *Binge eating: Nature, Assessment and Treatment*, edited by C. G. Fairburn and G. T. Wilson. New York: The Guilford Press.

Fairburn, C. G., S. L. Welch, H. A. Doll, B. A. Davies, and M. E. O'Connor. 1997. Risk factors for bulimia nervosa. A community-based, case-control study. *Archives of General Psychiatry* 54:509–517.

Favazza, A. R., and K. Conterio. 1988. The plight of chronic self-mutilators. *Community Mental Health* 24:22–30.

Favazza, A. R., L. DeRosear, and K. Conterio. 1989. Self-mutilation and eating disorders. *Suicide and Life-Threatening Behavior* 19:352–361.

Fluoxetine Bulimia Nervosa Collaborative Study Group. 1992. Fluoxetine in the treatment of bulimia nervosa: A multicenter, placebo-controlled, double-blind trial. *Archives of General Psychiatry* 49:139–147.

Frost, R. O., R. G. Heimberg, C. S. Holt, J. I. Mattia, and A. L. Neubauer. 1993. A comparison of two measures of perfectionism. *Personality and Individual Differences* 14:119–126.

Garfinkel P. E., E. Lin, P. Goering, C. Spegg, D. S. Goldbloom, S. Kennedy, A. S. Kaplan, and D. B. Woodside. 1995. Bulimia nervosa in a Canadian community sample: Prevalence and comparison of subgroups. *American Journal of Psychiatry* 152:1052–1058.

Garner, D. M., and P. E. Garfinkel. 1980. Sociocultural factors in the development of anorexia nervosa. *Psychological Medicine* 10:647–656.

Garner, D. M., and S. C. Wooley. 1991. Confronting the failure of behavioral and dietary treatments of obesity. *Clinical Psychology Review* 11:729–780.

Geller, J., C. Johnston, and K. Madsen. 1997. The role of shape and weight in self concept: The shape and weight based self-esteem inventory. *Cognitive Therapy and Research* 21:5–24.

Gendlin, E. 1978. *Focusing.* New York: Bantam Books.

Gleason, J. H., A. M. Alexander, and C. L. Somers. 2000. Later adolescents' reactions to three types of childhood teasing: Relations with self-esteem and body image. *Social Behavior and Personality* 28:471–480.

Godart, N. T., M. F. Flament, F. Perdereau, and P. Jeammet. 2002. Comorbidity between eating disorders and anxiety disorders: A review. *International Journal of Eating Disorders* 32:253–270.

Greenberger, D. and C. A. Padesky. 1995. *Mind over Mood: Changing the Way You Feel by Changing the Way You Think.* New York: The Guilford Press.

Hamachek, D. E. 1978. Psychodynamics of normal and neurotic perfectionism. *Psychology: A Journal of Human Behavior* 15:27–33.

Heatherton, T. F., M. Striepe, and L. Wittenberg. 1998. Emotional distress and disinhibited eating: The role of self. *Personality and Social Psychology Bulletin* 24:301–313.

Herman, C. P. and D. Mack. 1975. Restrained and unrestrained eating. *Journal of Personality* 43:647–660.

Herman, C. P., and J. Polivy. 1984. A boundary model for the regulation of eating. In *Eating and Its Disorders*, edited by A. J. Stunkard and E. Stellar. New York: Basic Books.

Herman, C. P., J. Polivy, and R. Silver. 1979. Effects of an observer on eating behavior: The induction of sensible eating. *Journal of Personality* 47:85–99.

Ingram, R. E., J. Miranda, and Z. V. Segal. 1998. *Cognitive Vulnerability to Depression*. New York: The Guilford Press.

Jacobson, N. S., C. R. Martell, and S. Dimidjian. 2001. Behavioral activation treatment for depression: Returning to contextual roots. *Clinical Psychology: Science and Practice* 8:255–270.

Jasper, K. 1993. Out from under body image disparagement. In *Consuming Passions*, edited by C. Brown and K. Jasper. Toronto: Second Story Press.

Jonas, J. M., M. S. Gold, D. Sweeney, and A. L. Pottash. 1987. Eating disorders and cocaine abuse: A survey of 259 cocaine abusers. *Journal of Clinical Psychiatry* 48:47–50.

Kabat-Zinn, J. 1990. *Full Catastrophe Living: Using the Wisdom of Your Body and Mind to Face Stress, Pain, and Illness*. New York: Dell Publishing.

———. 1994. *Wherever You Go, There You Are: Mindfulness Meditation in Everyday Life*. New York: Hyperion.

Keel, P. K., J. E. Mitchell, T. L. Davis, and S. J. Crow. 2001. Relationship between depression and body dissatisfaction in women diagnosed with bulimia nervosa. *International Journal of Eating Disorders* 30:48–56.

Keesey, R. E. 1993. Physiological regulation of body energy: Implications for obesity. In *Obesity: Theory and Therapy*. 2d ed. Edited by A. J. Stunkard and T. A. Wadden. New York: Raven Press.

Keys, A., J. Brozak, A. Henschel, O. Nickelsen, and H. L. Taylor. 1950. *The Biology of Human Starvation*. Minneapolis: University of Minnesota Press.

Lacey, J. H., and C. Evans. 1986. The impulsivist: A multi-impulsive personality disorder. *British Journal of Addiction* 81:715–723.

Lee, N. F., A. J. Rush, and J. E. Mitchell. 1985. Bulimia and depression. *Journal of Affective Disorders* 9:231–238.

Lilenfeld, L. R., W. H. Kaye, C. G. Greeno, K. R. Merikangas, K. Plotnicov, C. Pollice, R. Rao, M. Strober, C. M. Bulik, and L. Nagy. 1997. Psychiatric disorders in women with bulimia nervosa and their first-degree relatives: Effects of comorbid substance dependence. *International Journal of Eating Disorders* 22:253–264.

———. 1998. A controlled family study of anorexia nervosa and bulimia nervosa: Psychiatric disorders in first-degree relatives and effects of proband comorbidity. *Archives of General Psychiatry* 55:603–610.

Maloney, M. J., J. B. McGuire, S. R. Daniels, and B. Specker. 1988. Dieting behavior and eating attitudes in children. *Pediatrics* 84:482–489.

Marlatt, G. A., and D. Rohsenow. 1980. Cognitive processes in alcohol use: Expectancy and balanced placebo design. In *Advances in Substance Abuse: Behavioral and Biological Research*, edited by N. K. Mello. Greenwich, Conn.: JAI.

Marlatt, G. A., and J. R. Gordon. 1985. *Relapse Prevention: Maintenance Strategies in the Treatment of Addictive Behaviors.* New York: The Guilford Press.

McCabe, R. E., T. McFarlane, K. R. Blankstein, and M. P. Olmsted. 2000. Dimensions of perfectionism in individuals with eating disorders, dieters, and non-dieters. Paper presented at the Academy for Eating Disorders Ninth International Conference on Eating Disorders, New York.

McFarlane, T., J. Polivy, and C. P. Herman. 1998. Effects of false weight feedback on mood, self-evaluation, and food intake in restrained and unrestrained eaters. *Journal of Abnormal Psychology* 107:312–318.

Miller, W. R. and S. Rollnick. 2002. *Motivational Interviewing: Preparing People for Change.* 2d ed. New York: The Guilford Press.

Minuchin, S., L. Baker, B. L. Rosman, R. Lieberman, L. Milman, and T. C. Todd. 1975. A conceptual model of psychosomatic illness in children. *Archives of General Psychiatry* 32:1031–1038.

Mitchell, J. E., C. Pomeroy, and M. Huber. 1988. A clinician's guide to the eating disorders medicine cabinet. *International Journal of Eating Disorders* 7:211–223.

Mitchell, J. E., D. Hatsukami, R. L. Pyle, and E. D. Eckert. 1986. The bulimia syndrome: Course of the illness and associated problems. *Comprehensive Psychiatry* 27:165–170.

Mitchell, J. E., and M. de Zwaan. 1993. Pharmacological treatments of binge eating. In *Binge Eating: Nature, Assessment, and Treatment*, edited by C. G. Fairburn and G. T. Wilson. New York: The Guilford Press.

Molleken, L. 2000. Medications and eating disorders. *National Eating Disorder Information Centre Bulletin* 15(5).

Mynors-Wallis, L. M., and M. T. Hegel. 2000. *Problem-solving treatment for primary care: A treatment manual.* Unpublished manuscript.

Paul, T., K. Schroeter, B. Dahme, and D. O. Nutzinger. 2002. Self-injurious behavior in women with eating disorders. *American Journal of Psychiatry* 159:408–411.

Pike, K., K. Loeb, and K. Vitousek. 1996. Cognitive-behavioral therapy for anorexia nervosa and bulimia nervosa. In *Body Image, Eating Disorders, and Obesity*, edited by J. Kevin Thompson. Washington, D.C.: American Psychological Association.

Polivy, J., and C. P. Herman. 1976a. Clinical depression and weight change: A complex reaction. *Journal of Abnormal Psychology* 86:338–340.

———. 1976b. The effects of alcohol on eating behavior: Disinhibition or sedation? *Addictive Behaviors* 1:121–125.

Polivy, J., C. P. Herman, J. Younger, and B. Erskine. 1979. The effects of a model on eating behavior: The induction of a restrained eating style. *Journal of Personality* 47:100–117.

Polivy, J., C. P. Herman, R. Hackett, and I. Kuleshnyk. 1987. The effects of self-attention and public attention on eating in restrained and unrestrained subjects. *Journal of Personality and Social Psychology* 50:1253–1260.

Polivy, J., P. Herman, and T. McFarlane. 1994. Effects of anxiety on eating: Does palatability moderate distress-induced overeating in dieters? *Journal of Abnormal Psychology* 103:505–510.

Pomeroy, C., and J. E. Mitchell. 2002. Medical complications of anorexia nervosa and bulimia nervosa. In *Eating Disorders and Obesity*. 2d ed. Edited by C. G. Fairburn and K. D. Brownell. New York: The Guilford Press.

Prochaska, J. O., and C. C. DiClemente. 1982. Transtheoretical therapy: Toward a more integrative model of change. *Psychotherapy: Theory, Research, and Practice* 19:276–288.

Ricciardelli, L. A., and M. P. McCabe. 2001. Children's body image concerns and eating disturbance: A review of the literature. *Clinical Psychology Review* 21:325–344.

Rothwell, N. J., and M. J. Stock. 1979. A role for brown adipose tissue in diet-induced thermogenesis. *Nature* 281:31–35.

Ruderman, A. J. 1985. Dysphoric mood and overeating: A test of restraint theory's disinhibition hypothesis. *Journal of Abnormal Psychology* 94:78–85.

Schwalberg, M. D., D. H. Barlow, S. A. Alger, and L. J. Howard. 1992. Comparison of bulimics, obeses, binge eaters, social phobics, and individuals with panic disorders on comorbidity across *DSM-III-R* anxiety disorders. *Journal of Abnormal Psychology* 101:4675–4681.

Segal, Z. V., J. M. G. Williams, and J. D. Teasdale. 2002. *Mindfulness-Based Cognitive Therapy for Depression: A New Approach to Preventing Relapse*. New York: The Guilford Press.

Shafran, R., Z. Cooper, and C. G. Fairburn. 2002. Clinical perfectionism: a cognitive-behavioural analysis. *Behaviour Research and Therapy* 40:773–791.

Sims, E. A. H. 1976. Experimental obesity, diet-induced thermogenesis and their clinical implications. *Clinics in Endocrinology and Metabolism* 5:377–395.

Sims, E. A. H., R. F. Goldman, C. M. Gluck, E. S. Horton, P. C. Kelleher, and D. W. Rowe. 1968. Experimental obesity in man. *Transactions of the Association of American Physicians* 81:153–170.

Statistics Canada. 2001. National Population Health Survey. Ottawa, Ont.: Ministry of Industry and Canadian Institute for Health Information.

Steere, J., G. Butler, and P. J. Cooper. 1990. The anxiety symptoms of bulimia nervosa: A comparative study. *International Journal of Eating Disorders* 9:293–301.

Striegel-Moore, R. H., L. R. Silberstein, and J. Rodin. 1993. The social self in bulimia nervosa: Public self-consciousness, social anxiety, and perceived fraudulence. *Journal of Abnormal Psychology* 102:297–303.

Suyemoto, K. L. 1998. The functions of self-mutilation. *Clinical Psychology Review* 18:531–554.

Tiggemann, M., and E. Wilson-Barrett. 1998. Children's figure ratings: Relationship to self-esteem and negative stereotyping. *International Journal of Eating Disorders* 23:83–88.

Townsend, E., K. Hawton, D. G. Altman, E. Arensman, D. Gunnell, P. Hazell, A. House, and K. Van Heeringen. 2001. The efficacy of problem-solving treatments after deliberate self-harm: Meta-analysis of randomized controlled trials with respect to depression, hopelessness and improvement in problems. *Psychological Medicine* 31:979–988.

United States Department of Health and Human Services. 1997. FDA proposes safety measures for ephedrine dietary supplements. *Health and Human Services News Bulletin* June.

Urbszat, D., C. P. Herman, and J. Polivy. 2002. Eat, drink, and be merry, for tomorrow we diet: Effects of anticipated deprivation on food intake in restraint and unrestrained eaters. *Journal of Abnormal Psychology* 111:396–401.

Wells, A. 1997. *Cognitive Therapy of Anxiety Disorders: A Practice Manual and Conceptual Guide.* New York: John Wiley and Sons.

Welsh, S. O., C. Davis, and A. Shaw. 1993. *USDA's Food Guide: Background and Development.* Miscellaneous Publication No. 1514. United States Department of Agriculture. Washngton, D.C.: U.S. Government Printing Office.

Wiederman, M. W., and T. Pryor. 1996. Substance use among women with eating disorders. *International Journal of Eating Disorders* 20:163–168.

Woodside, B. D. 1993. Genetic contributions to eating disorders. In *Medical Issues and the Eating Disorders: The Interface,* edited by A. Kaplan and P. Garfinkel. New York: Brunner/Mazel.

Zhu, A. J., and B. T. Walsh. 2002. Pharmacologic treatment of eating disorders. *Canadian Journal of Psychiatry* 47:227–234.

Randi E. McCabe, Ph.D., C.Psych., worked for several years at the University Health Network, Toronto General Hospital Eating Disorders Programme, a world-renowned program in the field of eating disorder treatment. She has published chapters and articles on this subject and has presented at the Eating Disorder Research Society, an international conference for eating disorder researchers. She also maintains a private practice specializing in eating disorder treatment. She is a Staff Psychologist at St. Joseph's Healthcare and an Assistant Professor in the Department of Psychiatry and Behavioural Neurosciences at McMaster University in Hamilton, Ontario, Canada.

Traci L. McFarlane, Ph.D., C.Psych., is a Staff Psychologist at the University Health Network, Toronto General Hospital Eating Disorders Programme and an Assistant Professor in the Department of Psychiatry at the University of Toronto. She has presented at many North American and international conferences on the topic of eating disorders and has published chapters and articles in this area. She is also a CBT therapist on a National Institute of Mental Health study for preventing relapse in anorexia nervosa, conducted jointly by the University of Toronto and Columbia University.

Marion P. Olmsted, Ph.D., C.Psych., is the Director of the Ambulatory Care for Eating Disorders Programme at the University Health Network, Toronto General Hospital and an Associate Professor in the Department of Psychiatry at the University of Toronto. She is a well-known expert in the treatment of eating disorders and has presented at numerous international scientific meetings and published many articles and book chapters in this area. She is also a co-investigator and CBT therapy supervisor on a National Institute of Mental Health study for preventing relapse in anorexia nervosa, conducted jointly at the University of Toronto and Columbia University.

Some Other
New Harbinger Titles

The Cyclothymia Workbook, Item 383X, $18.95

The Matrix Repatterning Program for Pain Relief, Item 3910, $18.95

Transforming Stress, Item 397X, $10.95

Eating Mindfully, Item 3503, $13.95

Living with RSDS, Item 3554 $16.95

The Ten Hidden Barriers to Weight Loss, Item 3244 $11.95

The Sjogren's Syndrome Survival Guide, Item 3562 $15.95

Stop Feeling Tired, Item 3139 $14.95

Responsible Drinking, Item 2949 $18.95

The Mitral Valve Prolapse/Dysautonomia Survival Guide, Item 3031 $14.95

Stop Worrying Abour Your Health, Item 285X $14.95

The Vulvodynia Survival Guide, Item 2914 $15.95

The Multifidus Back Pain Solution, Item 2787 $12.95

Move Your Body, Tone Your Mood, Item 2752 $17.95

The Chronic Illness Workbook, Item 2647 $16.95

Coping with Crohn's Disease, Item 2655 $15.95

The Woman's Book of Sleep, Item 2493 $14.95

The Trigger Point Therapy Workbook, Item 2507 $19.95

Fibromyalgia and Chronic Myofascial Pain Syndrome, second edition, Item 2388 $19.95

Kill the Craving, Item 237X $18.95

Rosacea, Item 2248 $13.95

Thinking Pregnant, Item 2302 $13.95

Shy Bladder Syndrome, Item 2272 $13.95

Help for Hairpullers, Item 2329 $13.95

Coping with Chronic Fatigue Syndrome, Item 0199 $13.95

The Stop Smoking Workbook, Item 0377 $17.95

Multiple Chemical Sensitivity, Item 173X $16.95

Breaking the Bonds of Irritable Bowel Syndrome, Item 1888 $14.95

Parkinson's Disease and the Art of Moving, Item 1837 $16.95

The Addiction Workbook, Item 0431 $18.95

The Interstitial Cystitis Survival Guide, Item 2108 $15.95

Call **toll free, 1-800-748-6273,** or log on to our online bookstore at **www.newharbinger.com** to order. Have your Visa or Mastercard number ready. Or send a check for the titles you want to New Harbinger Publications, Inc., 5674 Shattuck Ave., Oakland, CA 94609. Include $4.50 for the first book and 75¢ for each additional book, to cover shipping and handling. (California residents please include appropriate sales tax.) Allow two to five weeks for delivery.

Prices subject to change without notice.